food to Die for

Secrets from

Kay Scarpetta's Kitchen

Patricia Cornwell

and Marlene Brown

LITTLE, BROWN AND COMPANY

A *Little, Brown* Book

First published in the United States in 2001 by G.P. Putnam's Sons

First published in Great Britain in 2001 by Little, Brown and Company

Copyright © 2001 by Cornwell Enterprises, Inc

The following titles from Patricia Cornwell: *Postmortem*, copyright © 1990;
Body of Evidence, copyright © 1991; *All That Remains*, copyright © 1992; *Cruel & Unusual*,
copyright © 1993; *The Body Farm*, copyright © 1994; *From Potter's Field*, copyright © 1995;
Cause of Death, copyright © 1996; *Unnatural Exposure*, copyright © 1997;
Point of Origin, copyright © 1998; *Black Notice*, copyright © 1999;
and *The Last Precinct*, copyright © 2000. Used by permission of
Little, Brown and Company (UK).

The moral right of the author has been asserted

*The recipes in this book are to be followed exactly as written. Neither the publisher nor the
author is responsible for specific health or allergy needs that may require medical supervision,
or for any adverse reactions to the recipes contained in this book.*

A CIP catalogue record for this book
is available from the British Library.

ISBN 0 316 85956 7

Book Design by BTDnc
Photography by Harry Chamberlain
Food Styling by Marlene Brown
Prop Styling by Kim Wong
Produced by The Philip Lief Group, Inc.

Printed and bound in Great Britain by
Butler & Tanner Ltd,
Frome and London

Little, Brown and Company (UK)
Brettenham House
Lancaster Place
London WC2E 7EN

www.littlebrown.co.uk

To

Cindy and Ed Bosker,
who gave me my first cooking job—
at the Peregrine House
in Davidson, North Carolina

Acknowledgments

Thank you, Jamie Saxon of The Philip Lief Group, for your clever book concept that brought Patricia and me together, along with your amazing vision and guidance through the entire project. To Patricia Cornwell, my heartiest thanks for sharing with me your warm hospitality, your mouth-watering words in a dozen novels' worth of Kay Scarpetta's cooking adventures, and also your most treasured stew and barbecued steak recipes! I was also privileged to be part of an extraordinary photographic team, with my friend and photographer Harry Chamberlain, prop stylist Kim Wong, and food styling assistant Carolyn Styler. Last but not least, many thanks to my husband and chief taster, John Oliphant, and to my mother, Lorraine Brown, who has always been my best editor.

—*Marlene Brown*

CONTENTS

The Body Farm

From Potter's Field

Cause of Death

Unnatural Exposure

Point of Origin

Black Notice

The Last Precinct

KILLER INGREDIENTS

COURSES

Starters

Funghi e Carciofì *(Mushroom and Artichoke Starter)*   92   From Potter's Field
Jumbo Shrimps with Bev's Kicked by a Horse
    Cocktail Sauce   174   Unnatural Exposure
Crostini di Polenta con Funghi Trifolati *(Grilled Polenta
    Topped with Sautéed Assorted Mushrooms)*   212   The Last Precinct

Soups

Miami-Style Chilli with Beer   58   All That Remains
Zuppa di Aglio Fresco *(Fresh Garlic Soup)*   78   The Body Farm
French Onion Soup   134   From Potter's Field
Rose's Vegetable Soup with Italian Herbs   194   Black Notice

Salads and Side Dishes

Wild Rice Salad with Cashews   62   Cruel & Unusual
Marinated Coleslaw with Apple Cider Vinaigrette   69   Cruel & Unusual
Linguine with Olive Oil, Parmesan and Onion   139   From Potter's Field
Fig, Melon and Prosciutto Salad   160   Cause of Death
Greek Salad with Red Wine Vinaigrette   186   Point of Origin
Salade de Gruyère *(Gruyère Salad)*   198   Black Notice
Giardinietto al Profumo di Erbe
    (Grilled Garden Vegetables)   215   The Last Precinct

Breads

Mrs. McTigue's Cheddar Cheese Biscuits 36	Body of Evidence
Hearty Seven-Grain Bread 66	Cruel & Unusual
Braided Country Bread 152	Cause of Death

Dinner Entrées

Pasta and Pizza

Italian Sausage Pizza with Peppers, Mushrooms and Onions 28	Postmortem
Le Pappardelle del Cantunzein *(Yellow and Green Broad Noodles with Sweet Peppers and Sausage)* 50	All That Remains
Kay's Fresh Pasta 52	All That Remains
Ravioli with Squash and Chestnut Filling 80	The Body Farm
Rigatoni con Broccolo *(Rigatoni with Broccoli)* 129	From Potter's Field
Tortellini Verdi *(Spinach Tortellini)* 136	From Potter's Field
Lasagne with Marinara Sauce and Porcini Mushrooms 146	Cause of Death
Kay's Marinara Sauce 150	Cause of Death
Lasagne coi Carciofi *(Lasagne with Artichokes and Béchamel Sauce)* 154	Cause of Death
Kay's Grilled Pizza with Sausage, Pepperoni and Three Cheeses 190	Black Notice

Fish and Seafood

Grilled Grouper with Butter and Key Lime Juice 64	Cruel & Unusual
Shrimp Sauté with Garlic and Lemon 90	From Potter's Field
Bev's Lump Crab Cakes 176	Unnatural Exposure
Lila's Clam Stew 178	Unnatural Exposure

Poultry

Pollo al Limone *(Lemon Chicken)*   94   From Potter's Field
Grilled Chicken Caesar Salad   184   Point of Origin

Meat

Grilled Marinated Rib-Eye Steaks   32   Postmortem
New York Steaks with Red Wine Marinade   42   All That Remains
Veal Breast Stuffed with Spinach Pistou   44   All That Remains
Pork Loin with Fig and Prosciutto Stuffing   47   All That Remains
Fruit-Marinated Lamb Kebabs   76   The Body Farm
Barbecued Baby Back Ribs   84   The Body Farm
Kay's Stew with Red Wine and Garlic   168   Unnatural Exposure
Costolette di Agnello alle Sette Erbe *(Lamb Chops
    Seasoned with Seven Herbs)*   217   The Last Precinct

Breakfast and Lunch Dishes

Omelette with Sweet Peppers and Onions   38   Body of Evidence
Fresh Fruit Salad with Blood Orange Dressing   162   Cause of Death
Classic English Breakfast *(Bacon and Eggs with
    Tomatoes and Mushrooms)*   164   Cause of Death
Marino's Breakfast Bagel Sandwich   182   Point of Origin
Marino's BLT on Rye   196   Black Notice

Desserts

Jack Daniel's Chocolate-Pecan Pie   86   The Body Farm
Madame Dugat's Mousse au Chocolat
    (Chocolate Mousse)   202   The Last Precinct
Lucy's Favourite Chocolate Chip Surprise Cookies   204   The Last Precinct
Peanut Butter-Chocolate Pie   206   The Last Precinct
Key Lime Meringue Pie   208   The Last Precinct

Introduction

F ood has many meanings for me. It is comfort, love, warmth, and
friendship. The essence of good cooking is generosity—not necessarily in
the size of the portion served, but in the giving of self to fill spaces in the
lives of others. When I cook for friends and family and occasionally when I
concoct something special just for myself, I'm trying to supply the hungry
spots—in both body and soul. When I invite people into my home, I want
them to feel happy and tended to. I mean it as a special gift when I say,
"Come over and I'll make pizza." When I return from a book-signing tour or
a research trip, I don't feel at home until my refrigerator is full and friends
are on their way over.

Using food to connect with others began when I was a child. The cookies
I made then for my neighbours are the ones that inspired the cookies Lucy
bakes in my novel *The Last Precinct*. I am warmed by recollections of
home-made soups before the fire in the split-log house that Ruth Graham
built. I treasure memories of Italian Christmas feasts at the home of Dr.
Marcella Fierro, the intrepid forensic pathologist who has always been my
mentor. When I sent home-made stew to my good friend Senator Orrin
Hatch, he called me and said it was the most wonderful thing he'd ever had
in his life. I knew it was my gesture—as much as the stew—that had fed a
deep emotional need in his exhausting, stressful life. It doesn't matter whether
every dish is a gourmet one; its true taste comes from the emotion of the
heart that inspired it and the effort of the hands that made it.

Many of the dishes I prepare for others as well as include in my novels
are related to healing and comfort. Of course, pasta is a fine medicine, and
you'll see many of my favourite pasta recipes in this book, including two

lasagnes. I call my *Pappardelle del Cantunzein* in *All That Remains* "mood food." Pasta is also love food. When you make fresh pasta, you're using your hands. Fresh pasta is light, warmth, and goodness all rolled together and created by touch. I included a Key lime pie for the Christmas dinner scene in *The Last Precinct* because I was inspired by memories of my grandmother, who had a Key lime tree that she allowed me to raid when I visited her in Florida. I would bootleg the limes back home, hoard the juice in the freezer, and make pies on special occasions. Even though I don't really like desserts and rarely eat them, I never turn down a pie made of real Key limes.

As I developed the character of Scarpetta, it was a natural and logical choice for me to decide that she loves to cook. I wanted her to be Italian because such a rich heritage adds a lushness to what for her is otherwise a stark, hard life. After Scarpetta puts her hands on death all day, she needs to come home to abundant beauty, wine, and delicious food with family and friends.

Her philosophy of cooking, like mine, is a blend of the diagnostic and generous. She cooks according to need, whether it is to create a mood or to supply energy or to cure what ails you. She "doctors" whatever she is putting together, and there are no rules. The final outcome justifies the means. Creative cook that she is, she can make do and make it special.

Like Scarpetta, I cook intuitively and sometimes whimsically. For example, I use olive oil and honey in my pizza crust. I didn't discover that combination in a recipe somewhere; I got the idea when I worked my way through college as the chief pizza-maker in the Peregrine House deli. One night when things were slow, I tried a little honey on a pizza crust because I had a hunch that it would be good. I have always had an instinct for knowing which ingredients will combine in a wonderful way: I imagine which ones will like each other, and the dish evolves in its own way.

I believe people should approach cooking with the heart and not as technicians. Become part of what you are creating instead of working to control it. Let it teach you instead of you telling it what to do. This is my philosophy of writing, and I learned long ago that if you let go, all that you lose are your limitations.

Many of my signature dishes, such as my Scarpetta Stew, never come out the same way twice. Each one has its own distinct personality, its own unique subtleties. The same is true of good wine, which speaks softly in a harmony of the distinctive tones that compose it. When I make stew, I begin with a huge pot and spend most of the day adding this and that, these and those. When I am really industrious, I pack containers of the finished product, home-made bread, and a nice Bordeaux or Burgundy into baskets that I give to special friends.

Many of my readers think I am Scarpetta. But I am all of my characters. So I can cook like Lucy and Marino, too. If you're not in the mood for home-made chicken soup with bay leaves and lots of sherry, then how about a breakfast bagel loaded with prosciutto, Gruyère, and slices of onion? What about a Reuben sandwich that is so sinful you need a bib?

Let me make one final and very important point before I turn you loose on my recipes. Just as a case is only as good as the evidence brought in, whatever you cook will either succeed or fail because of the ingredients you use. Be diligent about searching for cold-pressed extra-virgin olive oil and whole-milk buffalo mozzarella. Don't clear the scene until you've found fresh tomatoes, fresh garlic, and fresh herbs like basil and oregano. Don't let bad weather, fatigue, or distractions goad you into buying what's convenient or on special offer unless you are eating only to refuel. If you are cooking as a gift, spend a little extra money and take your time. Because what you offer others is also what you will receive.

In this book, which was initially conceived by Jamie Saxon and Marlene Brown, you will find recipes for all my favourite dishes as well as several from the restaurants that appear in my novels. I hope you will be inspired to cook from the heart and that you will enjoy both the process and the outcome. Bon appétit!

Zuppa di Aglio Fresco (Fresh Garlic Soup)

(PRECEDING PAGE) PAGE 168

Kay's Stew with Red Wine and Garlic

PAGE 136

Tortellini Verdi (Spinach Tortellini)

PAGE 202

Madame Dugat's Mousse au Chocolat

(Chocolate Mousse)

PAGE 198

Salade de Gruyère (Swiss Cheese Salad)

PAGE 28

Italian Sausage Pizza with
Peppers, Mushrooms, and Onions

PAGE 36

Mrs. McTigue's Cheddar Cheese Biscuits

(OVERLEAF) PAGE 162

Fresh Fruit Salad with Blood Orange Dressing

23

food to Die for

Postmortem

When all else fails, I cook.

Some people go out after a god-awful day and slam a tennis ball around or jog their joints to pieces on a fitness course. I had a friend in Coral Gables who would escape to the beach with her folding chair and burn off her stress with sun and a slightly pornographic romance she wouldn't have been caught dead reading in her professional world—she was a district court judge. Many of the cops I know wash away their miseries with beer at the FOP lounge.

I've never been particularly athletic, and there wasn't a decent beach within reasonable driving distance. Getting drunk never solved anything. Cooking was an indulgence I didn't have time for most days, and though Italian cuisine isn't my only love, it has always been what I do best.

"Use the finest side of the grater," I was saying to Lucy over the noise of water running in the sink.

"But it's so hard," she complained, blowing in frustration.

"Aged Parmigiano-Reggiano is hard. And watch your knuckles, okay?"

I finished rinsing green peppers, mushrooms, and onions, patted them dry, and placed them on the cutting board. Simmering on the stove was sauce made last summer from fresh Hanover tomatoes, basil, oregano, and several cloves of crushed garlic. I always kept a good supply in the freezer for times like these. Luganega sausage was draining on paper towels near other towels of browned lean beef. High-gluten dough was on the counter rising beneath a damp dish towel, and crumbled in a bowl was whole-milk mozzarella imported from New York and still packed in its brine when I'd bought it at my favorite deli on West Avenue. At room temperature the cheese is soft like butter, when melted is wonderfully stringy.

"Mom always gets the boxed kind and adds a bunch of junk to it," Lucy said breathlessly. "Or she buys the kind already made in the grocery store."

"That's deplorable," I retorted, and I meant it. "How can she eat such a thing?" I began to chop. "Your grandmother would have let us starve first."

My sister has never liked cooking. I've never understood why. Some of the happiest times when we were growing up were spent around the dinner table. When our father was well, he would sit at the head of the table and ceremoniously serve our plates with great mounds of steaming spaghetti or fettuccine or—on Fridays—frittata. No matter how poor we were, there was always plenty of food and wine, and it was always a joy when I came home from school and was greeted by delicious smells and promising sounds coming from the kitchen.

It was sad and a violation of tradition that Lucy knew nothing of these things. I assumed when she came home from school most days she walked into a quiet, indifferent house where dinner was a drudgery to be put off until the last minute. My sister should never have been a mother. My sister should never have been Italian.

Greasing my hands with olive oil, I began to knead the dough, working it hard until the small muscles in my arms hurt.

Italian Sausage Pizza with Peppers, Mushrooms and Onions

W hen all else fails, I cook," says Kay, well into the pages of Postmortem, *in reference to her personal coping strategies on a "god-awful" day. She doesn't consider herself much of an athlete, so she's not apt to go out jogging or dig out her tennis racket to shake off the day. But she does know Italian cuisine, and cooking is a head-clearing indulgence. What better way could there be to work out her frustrations than by greasing up her hands with olive oil and kneading her knuckles into a dough that is destined to become a pizza?*

Teaching a frustrated young Lucy how to grate the hard, well-aged Parmigiano-Reggiano cheese for the topping, Kay advises, "Use the finest side of the grater . . . And watch your knuckles, okay?" Her other favourite cheese, fresh whole-milk buffalo mozzarella, small balls of butter-soft cheese that float in liquid, is a New York import that Kay buys from her favourite Richmond deli on West Avenue. When she's in New York, she goes to Grace's Marketplace on the Upper East Side, at 1237 Third Avenue (71st Street). The mozzarella must be fully drained before using it to keep it from "weeping" into the pizza toppings. Kay tears the mozzarella into small, tantalizing bits that will melt like silk in the oven and become "wonderfully stringy" when a slice of just-baked pizza is put on the plate. If you've always gone for the hermetically sealed hunk of mozzarella from the cheese section of the supermarket, try the fresh—it will be a revelation.

For the sausage, Kay favours the sweet Italian Luganega, but your favourite sweet or spicy sausage will also do. Sometimes she also combines the sausage with well-browned, very lean minced beef. Bring out your extra-virgin olive oil, if you have it, to use in this recipe, and drizzle a little bit of it over the pizzas just before you bake them, à la Kay.

I worked in a pizza restaurant during my college years and one day hit on the idea of putting honey in my pizza dough. As it is for Kay, pizza is my great emergency food, and I always keep a stash of it in the freezer for quick meals. You can tightly wrap individual slices of the leftover pizza in foil, then place them in a tightly covered freezer container or self-sealing bag.

12 ounces/340 grams whole-milk mozzarella cheese (preferably fresh) or pre-grated mozzarella cheese

Pizza Crust:

18 to 19 ounces/510 to 540 grams high-gluten flour or strong plain white flour (see Note on page 31)

1 sachet fast action dry yeast

½ teaspoon salt

12 fluid ounces/340 millilitres very warm water (120° to 130°F/48° to 54°C)

1 tablespoon honey

1 tablespoon olive oil

Toppings:

2 tablespoons olive oil

2 green, red or yellow peppers, de-seeded and cut into 1-inch/2.5 centimetre pieces

3 ounces/85 grams fresh shiitake mushrooms, stems removed and caps chopped or 1 large portobello mushroom cap, chopped

12 ounces/340 grams sliced onions

4 cloves garlic, finely chopped

2 tablespoons chopped fresh basil

2 tablespoons chopped fresh oregano

Salt and freshly ground pepper

12 ounces/340 grams sweet Italian Luganega sausage or similar sweet or spicy sausage

16 fluid ounces/455 millilitres Kay's Marinara Sauce (page 150), prepared marinara sauce, or Quick Marinara Sauce (page 31)

2 ounces/55 grams freshly grated Parmigiano-Reggiano

1. At least 4 hours ahead or up to overnight, drain the liquid from the fresh mozzarella cheese, if using. Place the cheese in a strainer lined with a clean tea towel or a triple layer of kitchen paper, set over a large bowl, and place in the refrigerator to drain. Pat the cheese dry, then tear into small bits. Cover and refrigerate until needed.

2. For the crust: in a medium bowl, combine 15 ounces/425 grams of the flour, the yeast, and salt. Stir in the very warm water, honey, and olive oil, stirring until mixture begins to leave the sides of the bowl. Turn the dough out onto a lightly floured surface and gather it into a ball. Knead the dough for about 10 minutes, until it is soft, smooth, and elastic, adding enough of the remaining flour to keep the dough from sticking.

3. Place the dough in a large greased bowl and turn to coat evenly. Cover the dough with cling film or a damp, clean tea towel and place on the lowest oven rack. Turn the oven on to the lowest setting for 1 minute, then immediately turn the oven off. Let the dough rise for 30 to 40 minutes, or until doubled in size.

4. Punch the dough down. On a lightly floured surface, knead the dough ten times to release the air bubbles. Cut the dough in half and shape each piece into a ball. Cover the dough and let it rest while preparing the toppings.

5. For the toppings: in a large frying pan, heat the olive oil over medium-high

heat. Add the peppers, mushrooms, onions, and garlic and cook, stirring frequently, for about 5 minutes, or until the vegetables are tender. Stir in the basil and oregano; season with salt and pepper. Transfer the vegetable mixture to a large strainer set over a bowl to drain. Wipe the frying pan dry. In the same pan, crumble the sausage and cook over medium-high heat for about 8 minutes, or until browned. Transfer to kitchen paper to drain.

6. To assemble the pizzas: pre-heat oven to 450°F/230°C/gas mark 8. On a lightly floured surface, roll out or pat each piece of the dough into a 12-inch/30-centimetre round. Place each round on a lightly oiled baking sheet, pizza tin, or pizza baking stone. Spread half of the marinara sauce on each dough round; then sprinkle with half of the vegetable mixture, sausage, and Parmigiano-Reggiano. Top with the mozzarella.

7. Bake the pizzas (set the baking sheet or pizza tin on the lowest oven rack; set the pizza stone on the highest oven rack) for 10 to 13 minutes, or until the crust is golden brown and the cheese is beginning to brown. Cut into wedges and serve.

MAKES TWO 12-INCH/30-CENTIMETRE PIZZAS

NOTE: *To make high-gluten flour: place 15 ounces/425 grams plain flour in a large bowl. Add vital gluten powder (available in health food and speciality food shops) according to the package directions. Continue as directed in recipe.*

Variation

QUICK MARINARA SAUCE: In a medium bowl, combine 12 ounces/340 grams puréed tomatoes, 2 tablespoons chopped fresh basil, 1 tablespoon chopped fresh oregano, 1 teaspoon crushed fennel seeds, and salt and freshly ground pepper to taste.

Grilled Marinated Rib-Eye Steaks

Kay Scarpetta could never be a vegetarian, because she simply loves good meat, and she knows how to bring out all of its succulence over a flaming grill. For her grilled marinated steaks, she buys prime-grade beef rib-eye from her favourite butcher. Almost always the health-conscious cook, however, she carefully trims off all of the outside fat from the meat.

This unusual marinade, one of Kay's favourites, has a sweet flavour from honey. A range for the amount of honey has been given for cooks who prefer a little less sweetness and more of a barbecue flavour. Your favourite bottled barbecue sauce serves as the base for this marinade, and extra-virgin olive oil helps to round out the flavour. Because the recipe calls for top-quality steaks, just a short bath in the marinade, as little as 30 minutes, is necessary to imbue them with the honey-barbecue flavours. Avoid marinating longer than a couple of hours, or the meat will have a mushy texture when grilled.

Perhaps because she faces life-and-death situations daily, it's no surprise that Kay's grilling style involves pouring the marinade and the olive oil from an outstretched arm held high over the steaks while they are grilling. This method results in plenty of dramatic flames that require her to be quick on her feet (and can be dangerous to a less experienced grill master). The reward is steaks that cook up with beautifully charred crusts on the outside and are juicy pink on the inside. You can achieve the same sizzling results, with smaller and safer flames, by generously brushing the marinade and the olive oil directly onto the steaks with a long-handled barbecue brush. Kay serves these steaks with a red Bordeaux, a Burgundy, or a pinot noir.

4 beef rib-eye steaks (1 inch/2.5 centimetres thick, 10 ounces/280 grams
    each), trimmed of fat

16 fluid ounces/455 millilitres bottled barbecue sauce

4 to 8 fluid ounces/115 to 225 millilitres honey

3 tablespoons extra-virgin olive oil, plus additional for grilling

3 cloves garlic, finely chopped

1. Arrange the steaks in a shallow glass or ceramic dish In a large bowl, whisk together the barbecue sauce, honey (depending on desired sweetness), olive oil, and garlic until blended. Pour half of the mixture over the steaks, turning them over in the marinade to coat completely. Cover and refrigerate the steaks along with the remaining marinade (to be used later for basting the steaks), for at least 30 minutes or up to 2 hours.

2. To grill: Pre-heat the barbecue to medium-hot or pre-heat the grill. Drain the marinade from the steaks and discard. Pat the steaks dry with kitchen paper. Arrange the steaks on the grill directly over the hot coals, then generously baste the meat with the reserved marinade and some olive oil. Barbecue the steaks for 16 to 20 minutes for medium-rare (20 to 24 minutes for medium), brushing frequently with the marinade and olive oil, and turning the steaks once after 8 minutes. (Or place the steaks on the rack of a grill pan. Grill 4 inches/10 centimetres from the heat source, 9 to 10 minutes for medium-rare, turning them after 5 minutes.) The steaks will be charred on the outside and pink on the inside. Serve immediately on a warm platter.

SERVES 4

Mrs. McTigue's apartment was halfway down on the left, and my knock was promptly answered by a wizened woman with scanty hair tightly curled and yellowed like old paper. Her face was dabbed with rouge, and she was bundled in an oversize white cardigan sweater. I smelled floral-scented toilet water and the aroma of baking cheese.

"I'm Kay Scarpetta," I said.

"Oh, it's so nice of you to come," she said, lightly patting my offered hand. "Will you have tea or something a little stronger? Whatever you like, I have it. I'm drinking port."

All this as she led me into the small living room and showed me to a wing chair. Switching off the television, she turned on another lamp. The living room was as overwhelming as the set of the opera *Aïda*. On every available space of the faded Persian rug were heavy pieces of mahogany furniture: chairs, drum tables, a curio table, crowded bookcases, corner cupboards jammed with bone china and stemware. Closely spaced on the walls were dark paintings, bell pulls, and several brass rubbings.

She returned with a small silver tray bearing a Waterford decanter of port, two matching pieces of stemware, and a small plate arranged with homemade cheese biscuits. Filling our glasses, she offered me the plate and lacy linen napkins that looked old and freshly ironed. It was a ritual that took quite a long time.

Mrs. McTigue's Cheddar Cheese Biscuits

I n this scene from Body of Evidence, *Kay pays a visit to Mrs. J.R. McTigue, who was in charge of reservations for the Daughters of the American Revolution, where murder victim Beryl Madison spoke some months earlier. Mrs. McTigue serves Kay her freshly baked cheddar cheese biscuits, elegantly arranged on a silver tray with lace-rimmed linen napkins and cut-glass stemware filled with port.*

These miniature American biscuits, like little cheese scones, bake up with slightly crunchy edges and a flaky, butter-layered interior redolent of cheddar cheese. Keep in mind these secrets for mixing up light, flaky biscuits: when the butter is "cut in" (incorporated into the flour), make sure to cut the butter into successively smaller pieces, until they are no larger than small peas (a long-standing culinary phrase where pastry is concerned). The butter pieces must still be large enough to melt between the layers of dough during baking. You can use a pastry blender in a back-and-forth chopping motion in the mixing bowl, or two table knives scissor fashion.

Another secret is not to overwork the dough, because it is based on baking powder, not yeast, and therefore more delicate than bread dough. Knead the dough gently just a few times on a lightly floured surface, and roll it out with a few strokes of the rolling pin.

These biscuits bake up quickly and go well with a dinner or brunch menu, or with a salad lunch. If you prefer larger biscuits, simply use a 2-inch/5-centimetre biscuit cutter, and increase the baking time by 2 to 3 minutes.

10 ounces/280 grams plain flour

4 teaspoons baking powder

1 tablespoon sugar

1 teaspoon salt

$\frac{1}{2}$ teaspoon cream of tartar

3 ounces/85 grams cold unsalted butter, cut into pieces

5 ounces/140 grams finely shredded mature cheddar cheese

6 fluid ounces/170 millilitres milk

1. Pre-heat the oven to 425°F/220°C/gas mark 7. In a medium bowl, stir together the flour, baking powder, sugar, salt, and cream of tartar. Using a pastry blender or two knives scissor fashion, cut in the butter until the mixture resembles small peas.

2. Stir in the cheddar cheese. Add the milk all at once; stir the mixture until it is completely moistened.

3. Turn the dough out onto a generously floured board and gather it into a ball; knead about twelve times. With a rolling pin, roll the dough $\frac{1}{2}$ inch/1.25 centimetres thick. With a biscuit or cookie cutter, cut the dough into $1\frac{1}{2}$-inch/4-centimetre rounds. Place the rounds 1 inch/2.5 centimetres apart on a greased baking sheet.

4. Bake the biscuits for 10 to 12 minutes, or just until light golden brown. Serve hot.

| MAKES 3 DOZEN BISCUITS |

Omelette with Sweet Peppers and Onions

As the plot thickens in Body of Evidence, *Kay decides to cook a simple dinner for herself. As the story goes, it is an omelette that, unfortunately, she isn't destined to eat. But the great thing about omelettes is that they can be whipped up in no time—Kay often eats them for supper when she's tired from a day at the morgue. She fills them with vegetables, cheese, and even fruit. (At a restaurant once, I had an omelette filled with cream cheese and fig preserves for brunch, and it was wonderful.)*

An omelette pan, a small frying pan about 6 to 10 inches/15 to 25 centimetres in diameter, is a worthwhile investment for making delicious omelettes, especially if it is coated with a non-stick surface. Omelette pans have sloped sides that make it easy to move the omelette mixture around, and eventually, to flip it over its filling and slide it out of the pan.

Because omelettes cook so quickly, it's important to get the filling ready first. Then heat the oil in the pan until it is just hot enough to sizzle a drop of water. Kay prefers her omelettes well done, so she adds an extra flip: before spooning on the filling, she flips the cooked omelette over like a pancake to cook the other side until it's well done.

2 tablespoons olive oil

1½ ounces/45 grams de-seeded and chopped red yellow, or green pepper

1½ ounces/45 grams chopped onion

1 clove garlic, finely chopped

1 tablespoon chopped fresh basil

Salt and freshly ground pepper

2 very large eggs

2 tablespoons water

2 ounces/55 grams coarsely shredded mature cheddar, Emmental,
Gruyère or mozzarella

1. In an omelette pan or a small frying pan, heat 1 tablespoon of the oil over medium-high heat. Add the pepper, onion, and garlic, and cook, stirring frequently, for 3 to 5 minutes, until very tender. Stir in the basil and season with salt and pepper. Transfer the vegetables to a plate; cover and set aside.

2. In a small bowl, whisk together the eggs and water; season with salt and pepper. Heat the remaining 1 tablespoon olive oil in the same pan over medium-high heat until hot. Pour in the egg mixture all at once.

3. With a metal spatula, gently push the cooked parts of the omelette towards the centre of the pan, allowing the uncooked portion of egg to flow underneath. Tilt the pan and continue moving the cooked portion of egg as necessary, until the egg thickens and no liquid remains.

4. When the underside of the omelette begins to brown (use a table knife or narrow metal spatula to lift the edge of the omelette to check it), spoon the vegetable mixture onto one half of the omelette. Sprinkle with half of the cheese. With a spatula, fold the omelette in half or roll one side of the omelette over the filling.

5. To serve, invert the omelette onto a dinner plate or slide it onto the plate by tilting the pan. Sprinkle the omelette with the remaining cheese and serve immediately.

SERVES 1

pring lamb with white wine, breast of veal, or roast pork would be perfect." I filled a pot with water and set it on the stove. "I'm pretty amazing with lamb, but I'll have to give you a rain check."

"Maybe you ought to forget cutting up dead bodies and open a restaurant."

"I'll assume you mean that as a compliment."

"Oh, yeah." His face was expressionless, and he was lighting a cigarette. "So what do you call this?" He nodded at the stove.

"I call it yellow and green broad noodles with sweet peppers and sausage," I replied, adding the sausage to the sauce. "But if I really wanted to impress you, I would call it *le pappardelle del Cantunzein.*"

"Don't worry. I'm impressed."

"Marino." I glanced over at him. "What happened this morning?"

He replied with a question, "You mention to anyone what Vessey told you about the hack mark's being made with a serrated blade?"

"So far, you're the only person I've told."

"Hard to figure how Hilda Ozimek came up with that, with the hunting knife with a serrated edge she claims popped into her mind when Pat Harvey took her to the rest stop."

"It is hard to understand," I agreed, placing pasta in the boiling water. "There are some things in life that can't be reasoned away or explained, Marino."

Fresh pasta takes only seconds to cook, and I drained it and transferred it to a bowl kept warm in the oven. Adding the sauce, I tossed in butter and grated fresh Parmesan, then told Marino we were ready to eat.

"I've got artichoke hearts in the refrigerator." I served our plates. "But no salad. I do have bread in the freezer."

"This is all I need," he said, his mouth full. "It's good. Real good."

New York Steaks with Red Wine Marinade

When Washington Post *police reporter Abby Turnbull comes to Richmond, Kay invites her for dinner. It's a great excuse to escape her office at the morgue and head out to her favourite market to plan the menu. Selecting two perfect steaks, she decides that even these choice morsels can be improved greatly by one of her own special marinades. A simple mix of dry red wine, extra-virgin olive oil, and crushed fresh garlic works its magic on the meat, while Kay scrubs down the grill. Kay prefers her steaks medium-rare, with a lot of pink inside, so timings are given for both medium-rare and medium. Add a couple of minutes to the grilling time if you prefer to see only a hint of pink inside the meat.*

For a crisp accompaniment, Kay's favourite choice is a side salad composed of Boston lettuce leaves, mushrooms, sweet onions, and locally grown Hanover tomatoes, tossed together with a bottled blue cheese dressing.

4 New York strip (sirloin) steaks (1 inch/2.5 centimetres thick, 10 ounces/280 grams each), trimmed of fat

12 fluid ounces/340 millilitres dry red wine

2 fluid ounces/55 millilitres extra-virgin olive oil, plus additional for grilling

4 cloves garlic, crushed

2 bay leaves

Salt and freshly ground pepper

1. Arrange the steaks in a shallow glass or ceramic dish. In a medium bowl, whisk together the red wine, olive oil, garlic, bay leaves, and salt and pepper to taste. Pour the mixture over the steaks and turn the steaks over to coat them with the marinade. Cover and refrigerate for at least 1 hour or up to 4 hours.

2. To grill the steaks: pre-heat the barbecue to medium-hot or pre-heat the grill. Pour off the marinade from the meat and discard. Pat the steaks dry with kitchen paper. Lightly brush the steaks on both sides with some olive oil. Place them directly over the hot coals and barbecue for 18 to 22 minutes for medium-rare (20 to 24 minutes for medium), turning them once and brushing with additional olive oil. (Or place the steaks on the rack of a grill pan. Grill 4 inches/10 centimetres from the heat source for 8 to 10 minutes for medium-rare; 12 to 14 minutes for medium)

3. Season with salt and pepper. Serve immediately on a warm platter.

SERVES 4

Veal Breast Stuffed with Spinach Pistou

An elegant breast of veal, rolled and sliced to display a pinwheel of fragrant basil and spinach stuffing, is a special entrée for cooks who want something extra special for their dinner guests. A veal breast is unusual enough to warrant ordering one from your favourite butcher. Ask to have the breast boned, and have the butcher make a "pocket" in the meat for you. The pocket will be a deep slit in the long side of the breast, which makes it easy to stuff the meat.

The French word pistou *actually refers to a version of Italian pesto, made without the traditional pine nuts. Kay's is a combination of a French-style pistou of basil, garlic, and olive oil purée, mixed with sautéed mushrooms, onions, spinach, and breadcrumbs for a stuffing that promises to wind its way deliciously through the meat. Slathered inside the veal pocket, the stuffing can be corralled by sewing up the opening with a standard needle and thread, using large loose stitches that can easily be seen after roasting for quick removal. (Sterilize a household sewing needle with a flaming match.) Not surprisingly, Kay is good at this.*

Bake the veal roast uncovered at first to give it some colour. Avoid making the red wine sauce overly salty by opting for tinned low-sodium beef stock, and season the sauce with salt and pepper.

Spinach Pistou Stuffing:

1 ounce/25 grams loosely packed fresh basil, plus leaves for garnish

2 tablespoons snipped fresh chives

6 cloves garlic, finely chopped

1 very large egg

4 tablespoons olive oil

1 teaspoon salt

¼ teaspoon freshly ground pepper

3 ounces/85 grams chopped fresh mushrooms

3 ounces/85 grams chopped onion

3 ounces/85 grams fresh breadcrumbs

10 ounces/280 grams frozen chopped spinach, thawed and
  squeezed dry

Veal and Sauce:

1 (3½ to 4-pound/1.6 to 1.8 kilograms) veal breast, boned and with a pocket

Salt and freshly ground pepper

12 fluid ounces/340 millilitres dry red or white wine

16 fluid ounces/455 millilitres home-made beef stock or ready-made low
  sodium beef stock

6 ounces/170 grams finely chopped onions

3 tablespoons cornflour

1 tablespoon tomato purée

1. To make the pistou: in a food processor or blender, combine the basil, chives, garlic, egg, 2 tablespoons of the oil, salt, and pepper. Purée the mixture until it is smooth.

2. In a small frying pan, heat the remaining 2 tablespoons of oil over medium-high heat. Add the mushrooms and onion and cook, stirring frequently, for 3 to 5 minutes, until the vegetables are tender but not browned. In a large

bowl, toss together the breadcrumbs, spinach, mushroom mixture, and basil purée until combined.

3. Preheat the oven to 325°F/170°C/gas mark 3. On a large work surface, place the veal breast with the pocket side facing you. Spoon the pistou stuffing into the pocket, spreading it evenly along the length of the meat and keeping it away from the cut edge. Close the pocket by sewing it up with large loose stitches with a standard sewing needle and white thread. Starting at one of the short ends of the meat, roll up the roast, as tightly as you can, and place it seam-side down. Tie up the roast with kitchen string.

4. Transfer the roast to a large shallow roasting tin. Season with salt and pepper. Pour the red wine and 12 fluid ounces/340 millilitres of the beef stock over the roast. Sprinkle the onions around the meat.

5. Bake, uncovered, for 40 minutes. Cover the roasting tin tightly with aluminium foil. Bake for 1 to 1$\frac{1}{2}$ hours longer, or until the meat is tender when pierced with a fork, basting the meat occasionally with the drippings.

6. Transfer the meat to a chopping board; cover and keep warm. Strain the meat juices into a measuring cup; spoon off the fat. Add enough water to the meat juices to equal 1 pint/570 millilitres, if needed. Stir the cornflour into the remaining 4 fluid ounces/115 millilitres beef stock. In a 3$\frac{1}{2}$-pint/2-litre saucepan, stir together the meat juices, beef stock mixture, 4 fluid ounces/115 millilitres water, and the tomato purée. Bring the mixture to the boil over medium-high heat, stirring constantly. Reduce the heat and simmer, stirring frequently, for 1 to 2 minutes until the mixture thickens. Cook 2 minutes longer; taste and season with salt and pepper, if desired.

7. Untie the roast and remove the stitches. Cut the meat into $\frac{1}{2}$-inch-/1.25-centimetre thick slices and arrange on a warm platter. Garnish with some fresh basil leaves and serve the sauce alongside.

SERVES 8

Pork Loin with Fig and Prosciutto Stuffing

I f you're intimidated by the prospect of cooking a roast, you will find that a boneless pork loin is perhaps the easiest cut of all. It actually consists of two sides of the loin that have been boned and tied with their flat sides drawn together in one neat package. The result is a neat cylinder of pork that, once roasted, can be easily sliced from one end. There is very little fat on this roast.

Kay loves this savoury stuffing of dried figs, sautéed prosciutto, and onions. Slices of the finished roast reveal ribbons of the filling.

During roasting, watch that the top crust of the roast does not become too dark. Cover the roast loosely with a piece of aluminium foil when it gets to a nice golden brown stage. Pork is very lean and prone to drying out easily when overcooked, so use a meat thermometer, inserting it into the centre of the roast. Pork is done at 160°F/70°C, but it continues to cook for a few minutes after roasting. So remove it at 150° to 155°F/65° to 68°C, and the temperature will catch up while you are preparing the sauce.

The glistening port wine sauce gets its stunning looks and flavour from the meat juices and port wine. Since all of the alcohol cooks away in the saucepan, everyone at your table should be able to enjoy it. Kay's guests always do.

Fig and Prosciutto Stuffing:

1 tablespoon olive oil
2 ounces/55 grams chopped onion

3 ounces/85 grams chopped dried figs or prunes

3 ounces/85 grams chopped prosciutto

Roast:

1 tablespoon chopped fresh sage

1 tablespoon chopped fresh thyme

1 teaspoon salt

¼ teaspoon ground allspice

1 (4 to 4½-pound/1.8 to 2 kilograms) boneless pork loin roast, tied

Sauce:

3 tablespoons cornflour

16 fluid ounces/455 millilitres home-made beef stock or ready-made
    beef stock

2 fluid ounces/55 millilitres dry port

2 teaspoons chopped fresh thyme

Salt and freshly ground pepper

1. For the stuffing: In a medium frying pan, heat the oil over medium-high heat. Add the onion and cook for 3 to 5 minutes, or until tender and translucent. Stir in the figs or prunes and prosciutto; cook for 2 minutes longer. Remove from the heat.

2. Pre-heat the oven to 350°F/180°C/gas mark 4. In a small bowl, stir together the sage, thyme, salt, and allspice. Set aside.

3. Place the pork roast, with a long side facing you, on a chopping board. (Do not untie the roast.) With a sharp knife, make vertical cuts about 4 inches/10 centimetres long and 3 inches/8 centimetres deep, at ½-inch/1.25-centimetre intervals across the top of the roast. Spoon 1 tablespoon of the stuffing mixture into each slit, packing it in with the back of a teaspoon.

4. Place the roast on a rack in a shallow roasting tin. Rub the sage mixture generously over the roast. Roast the pork, uncovered, for 1 hour. Cover the

roast loosely with aluminium foil and roast for 20 to 40 minutes longer, or until the juices run clear when the meat is pierced and a meat thermometer inserted into the centre of the meat registers 150° to 155°F/65° to 68°C (temperature will increase to 160°F/70°C during standing).

5. Transfer the meat to a carving board; cover and keep warm.

6. For the Port Wine Sauce: pour the meat juices into a strainer set over a measuring cup, scraping up the crusty browned bits from the bottom of the tin. Skim off the fat. Add enough water to the meat juices to equal 5 fluid ounces/140 millilitres liquid, if necessary. Pour into a 3½-pint/2-litre saucepan. Whisk the cornflour into the beef stock to avoid lumps; stir into the meat juices with the port and thyme. Bring the mixture to the boil over medium-high heat, stirring. Reduce the heat to low and simmer, uncovered, for 2 minutes. Season with salt and pepper.

7. To serve, untie the roast and carefully slice it crosswise between the stuffing pockets into ½-inch-/1.25-centimetre-thick slices, to retain some of the stuffing in each slice. Arrange the slices on a warm platter. Serve with the sauce.

SERVES 8 TO 10

Le Pappardelle del Cantunzein

(Yellow and Green Broad Noodles with Sweet Peppers and Sausage)

Kay prepares this colorful Italian dish for Marino, serving it with a bottle of Mondavi red. Pappardelle, 3/4-inch-/2-centimetre-wide Italian noodles, can easily be made from Kay's Fresh Pasta.

SHORTCUT TIP: *No time to make home-made pasta? Purchase sheets of fresh spinach and egg pasta, or a high-quality dried pasta from an Italian deli or speciality food store.*

½ recipe Kay's Fresh Spinach Pasta (page 55), 12 ounces/340 grams store-bought fresh spinach pasta sheets, or 8 ounces/225 grams dried wide spinach noodles

½ recipe Kay's Fresh Pasta (page 52), 12 ounces/340 grams store-bought fresh egg pasta sheets, or 8 ounces/225 grams dried wide plain noodles

1 to 1¼ pounds/450 to 565 grams sweet Italian sausage

2 to 3 tablespoons olive oil

1 red pepper, thinly sliced

1 yellow pepper de-seeded and thinly sliced

6 ounces/170 grams sliced onions

3 cloves garlic, finely chopped

12 ounces/340 grams peeled (if desired), de-seeded, and coarsely chopped tomatoes

2 tablespoons chopped fresh basil, plus leaves for garnish

½ teaspoon salt

¼ teaspoon freshly ground pepper

1 tablespoon butter (optional)

1½ ounces/45 grams freshly grated Parmigiano-Reggano, plus
  additional for serving

1. *If making Kay's Fresh Pasta:* roll out 2 balls (½ of recipe) of spinach pasta dough and 2 balls of plain pasta dough as directed in the recipe. Dry the pasta sheets for 30 minutes. Put the pasta sheets on a chopping board and cut into ¾-inch-/2-centimetre-wide noodles. Separate the noodles and allow to dry for 2 hours. (Or cover noodles with cling film or a clean tea towel and let dry up to 24 hours.) Set aside. *If using store-bought fresh pasta sheets:* place each pasta sheet on a lightly floured chopping board. Cut into ¾-inch-/2-centimetre-wide strips and allow to dry as directed above.

2. In a large frying pan, crumble and cook the Italian sausage over medium-high heat for about 8 minutes or until browned and thoroughly cooked. Drain the sausage well; place a double layer of kitchen paper over sausage and press out excess fat. Wipe out the frying pan. In the same pan, heat 2 tablespoons of the olive oil over medium-high heat; add the red and yellow peppers, onions, and garlic and cook, stirring frequently, for about 5 minutes, until tender.

3. Stir in the sausage, tomatoes, basil, salt, and pepper; cover and simmer over medium-low heat for 10 minutes. Keep hot.

4. Meanwhile, cook pasta. *For Kay's noodles or store-bought fresh pasta sheets:* in a large pan, bring 6½ pints/4 litres of salted water to the boil. Add the noodles and cook for 2 to 3 minutes, or until *al dente* (tender but still firm to the bite). Drain. *For packaged dry pasta:* cook according to the package directions; drain.

5. To serve, transfer the noodles to a large platter. Toss the pasta with the butter, if desired. Spoon the hot sausage mixture over the pasta. Sprinkle with the Parmigiano-Reggiano and garnish with basil leaves.

SERVES 4

Kay's Fresh Pasta

When Kay has the time, she uses it wisely—to make her own pasta. This recipe gives you two options: a hand-rolling and cutting method, and a pasta-machine method. Is making fresh pasta really worth it? Think about the difference between store-bought and home-made bread. What do you think Kay would say?

15 ounces/425 grams unbleached plain flour
3 very large eggs, lightly beaten
2½ fluid ounces/70 millilitres water
2 teaspoons olive oil

1. Put 12½ ounces/355 grams of the flour into a large bowl; make a well in the centre with the back of a spoon. Pour the eggs, water, and olive oil into the well. Stir until all the flour is moistened, and it leaves the side of the bowl.

2. Turn the dough out onto a lightly floured surface and gather it into a ball. Knead the dough for about 10 minutes, until it is smooth and elastic, adding as much of the remaining flour as needed to keep the dough from sticking. (Too much added flour will result in a more brittle pasta when it dries.)

3. Shape the dough into a ball, then cut it into quarters. Shape each quarter into a ball; place each in a self-sealing plastic bag or wrap each one tightly in cling film. Allow the dough to rest for 30 minutes or refrigerate for up to 24 hours.

4. Roll and cut the pasta using the Hand-Rolling or Pasta-Machine Method (below). Dry the cut noodles as directed.

5. To cook the pasta: in a large pan, bring $6\frac{1}{2}$ pints/4 litres salted water to the boil. Cook freshly made pasta for 2 minutes; cook pasta that has been stored for more than a few days for 5 to 6 minutes, until *al dente* (tender but still firm to the bite). Drain, but do not rinse.

MAKES ABOUT $1\frac{1}{3}$ POUNDS/620 GRAMS FRESH PASTA,
ENOUGH FOR 8 SIDE-DISH OR 4 MAIN-DISH SERVINGS

HAND-ROLLING AND CUTTING METHOD:

Working with one ball (one-quarter) of the pasta dough at a time, place the dough on a lightly floured surface and flatten it into a round with the palm of your hand. With a rolling pin, roll the dough into a 15x10-inch/38x25-centimetre rectangle, frequently lifting the dough, turning it over, and lightly flouring the surface to prevent the dough from sticking. The dough should be $\frac{1}{8}$- to $\frac{1}{16}$-inch/3- to 1.5-millimetres thick (the thinner the dough, the more tender the pasta). If the dough is very elastic and difficult to roll, cover it and allow it to rest for 10 minutes, then continue rolling.

Spread several large pieces of greaseproof paper or a few clean tea towels on a work surface. Transfer the pasta sheet to the paper or towels. Roll out the remaining pieces of dough. Allow the pasta to air dry for 30 minutes. With a sharp knife or pizza cutter, cut the dough into $\frac{1}{8}$-inch-/3-millimetre-wide strips for linguine, $\frac{1}{4}$-inch-/6-millimetre-wide strips for fettuccine, 2-inch/5-centimetre-wide strips for lasagne noodles, or as desired. Separate the noodles and allow them to dry on the greaseproof paper or tea towels for at least 30 minutes or up to 2 hours. (To hold the pasta longer, cover it with cling film and dry at room temperature for up to 24 hours.)

HAND-CRANKED PASTA-MACHINE METHOD:

Working with one ball (one-quarter) of the pasta dough at a time, place the dough on a lightly floured surface. Flatten the dough into a round with the palm of your hand. Lightly flour the top of the dough. Set the rollers of the machine at their widest opening. Run dough through the machine two times. Cut the dough crosswise in half; set one piece aside.

Adjust the rollers to the next setting. Run one piece of the dough through the machine two times, catching the dough as it passes through (be careful not to allow the dough to fold back on itself), and lightly flouring the dough on both sides as necessary. Repeat, adjusting the rollers to successively smaller openings. (If the dough becomes too long and cumbersome to handle, cut it crosswise in half.) When the rollers are set to their smallest opening, run the dough through only one time.

Spread several large pieces of greaseproof paper or clean tea towels on a work surface. Transfer the pasta sheet to the paper or towels. Allow the pasta to dry for 30 minutes. Select the desired pasta cutter on the machine and cut the pasta according to the manufacturer's directions. Separate the noodles and allow them to dry on the paper or towels or on a standing pasta dryer for at least 30 minutes, or up to 2 hours. (To hold the pasta longer, cover it with cling film and dry at room temperature for up to 24 hours.)

TO STORE PASTA DOUGH:

Place each ball of pasta dough in a separate self-sealing plastic bag or wrap individually in cling film and refrigerate until needed, up to 1 day. To freeze, wrap each pasta ball in cling film and pack into airtight freezer containers; freeze for up to 1 month. Thaw overnight in the refrigerator before using.

For pasta that has been dried for 2 hours, stack the sheets between layers of greaseproof paper on a baking sheet and wrap airtight in cling film. Store at room temperature for up to several days. Completely dried, cut pasta can be stored in an airtight container at room temperature for up to 2 days.

Variation

KAY'S FRESH SPINACH PASTA: This dough is a little sticky, so be sure to keep the dough lightly sprinkled with flour during the rolling and cutting.

2 ounces/55 grams coarsely chopped fresh spinach leaves

2 very large eggs

15 ounces/425 grams plain flour

6 to 7 tablespoons water

1 teaspoon olive oil

In a blender or food processor, combine the spinach and 1 egg; cover and blend until puréed. Put 12½ ounces/355 grams of the flour into a large bowl; make a well in the centre with the back of a spoon. Add the spinach purée, the remaining egg, 6 tablespoons of the water, and the olive oil. Stir until the mixture is well blended. If it seems dry, add the remaining 1 tablespoon water and mix until the dough leaves the side of the bowl. Continue with Step 2 of Kay's Fresh Pasta (page 52).

The Quintessential Ingredient of Italian Cooking

Drizzled over fresh oven-baked crusty bread, whisked into the perfect vinaigrette, mingling with onions and peppers in a sauté—oh, the taste, the aroma! There is no question about it, good olive oil imparts a distinct flavour that defines Italian cuisine. How has olive oil come to be equated with great Italian cooking? About 98 per cent of the world's olive oil is produced in the Mediterranean region in and around Italy.

Like wine, olive oils vary considerably in flavour and quality. Climate and soil conditions, as well as the method of processing the oils, are factors that impart distinctive flavours, ranging from delicate to semi-fruity to a full-blown olive flavour. Colours vary from palest yellow to vivid dark green. Some olive oils are actually masterful blends of several varieties, so it becomes impossible to generalize about flavour when it comes to a dark-coloured oil vs. a light-coloured oil, for example.

Types of Olive Oils

Olive oil is made from pressed olives, and most of it comes from a single pressing. Some processors use heat and/or solvents to make the process more efficient. Kay Scarpetta prefers "cold-pressed" olive oils made in the age-old Italian tradition, without the use of heat or solvents. As you experiment with cooking Italian dishes, try a variety of these olive oils:

EXTRA-VIRGIN: The best olive oil you can buy and also the priciest. Made from the highest-grade olives, the oil comes from a single cold pressing. Natural sediments are carefully filtered out. By law, the acidity level must be less than 1 per cent. Use extra-virgin oils when the flavour will be most prominent, as in pasta dishes, marinades and sauces, salad dressings, and for basting meats, poultry, and fish or for dipping crusty breads. You'll savour every bite.

FINE VIRGIN: The next best thing to extra-virgin, with an allowable acidity level of

1.5 per cent. Fine virgin olive oil has a superior flavour and aroma and is an excellent choice for all of the same uses as extra-virgin oil.

VIRGIN: Still superior in quality and smooth in flavour. The allowed acidity level is 3.3 per cent. A good-quality virgin olive oil is for any recipe, especially where a lighter taste is desired, and it can also be used for sautéing and stir-frying.

PURE: Sometimes called "classic," this is a good general-purpose olive oil that is well suited to everything from salad dressings and sauces to sautéing and stir-frying. Pure olive oils have been refined to remove most of the impurities, which also removes some of the flavour and colour. The better pure olive oils have some extra-virgin or virgin oils blended in to add back some of the flavour.

LIGHT OR EXTRA LIGHT: These terms have nothing to do with calories; these are highly refined oils with a very mild flavour, colour, and aroma. Use as you would any plain vegetable oil, but don't look for this in Kay's kitchen.

POMACE: This is the least expensive olive oil, made by extracting additional oil from the pomace, the portion of the olive that is left after the mechanical pressing. This oil may be blended with a small amount of virgin olive oil, but don't let that impress you. This oil is lowest in terms of the grand order of quality olive oil.

Storing Olive Oil

A very good quality olive oil stores well when it's kept in a cool dark place. Extra-virgin oils keep well up to two years if properly stored, but use pure oil within one year. If the weather is hot or humid, olive oils can be stored in the refrigerator, but once opened should be used within a few months. Some clouding of the oil might occur in the refrigerator, but neither the flavour nor the quality will be affected. The oil will clear up once it's brought to room temperature – a good idea before using oils that have been chilled. Check your oil after it has been stored for a while. An off-odour or taste or a change in colour will tell you it's past its prime.

Miami-Style Chilli with Beer

Anna, a friend of Kay's, invites Kay over to her house for dinner. Anna cooks up this chilli with cans of chillies and garlic-spiked tomatoes that Kay brought home from her last visit to Miami. This chilli has the consistency of soup and is pleasantly spicy, since Kay uses the tame green (Anaheim) variety of chillies. However, you can crank up the heat by adding more chilli powder and by passing a bottle of hot pepper sauce around the table.

Corona and Dos Equis are popular Mexican beers that will lend great flavour to this chilli. If you have leftover chilli, it freezes very well. Use airtight freezer containers, leaving $^1/_2$ inch/1.25 centimetres headspace at the top for expansion.

1 pound/450 grams lean minced turkey or extra-lean minced beef

3 tablespoons olive oil

3 ounces/85 grams trimmed and sliced mushrooms

9 ounces/255 grams de-seeded and chopped green, red or yellow peppers

6 ounces/170 grams chopped onions

2 cloves garlic, finely chopped

2 tins (28 ounces/790 grams each) chopped tomatoes with diced green chillies

2 tins (16 ounces/450 grams each) red kidney beans, rinsed and well drained

1 tin (16 ounces/450 grams) black beans, rinsed and well drained

1 bottle (12 fluid ounces/340 mililitres) Mexican beer

3 tablespoons red wine vinegar

2 tablespoons chopped fresh oregano or marjoram

2 tablespoons chopped fresh basil

2 bay leaves

1 1/2 tablespoons chilli powder

2 teaspoons salt

1 1/2 teaspoons ground cumin

Coarsely grated mature cheddar cheese, for garnish

1. In a large flameproof casserole dish or large saucepan, cook the minced turkey or beef in 1 tablespoon of the olive oil over medium-high heat for about 5 minutes, or until browned, breaking up the meat with the side of a spoon. Drain the meat well. Transfer to a double layer of kitchen paper and press out the excess fat. Wipe out the pan.

2. In the same pan, heat the remaining 2 tablespoons olive oil over medium-high heat. Add the mushrooms, peppers, onions, and garlic and cook, stirring frequently, for 5 minutes, until the peppers are tender. Stir in the meat, tomatoes with their juices, the kidney and black beans, beer, vinegar, oregano or marjoram, basil, bay leaves, chilli powder, salt, and cumin. Bring the mixture to the boil. Reduce the heat to medium-low and simmer, partially covered, for 1 1/2 hours, stirring occasionally.

3. Taste the chilli for seasoning. Remove the bay leaves. To serve, ladle the chilli into bowls and top each serving with cheddar cheese.

SERVES 8 TO 10

She pushed back her chair and got up. "I hope you're hungry. We've got chicken breasts and a chilled wild rice salad made with cashews, peppers, sesame oil. And there's bread. Is your grill in working order?"

"It's after eleven and snowing outside."

"I didn't suggest that we eat outside. I simply would like to cook the chicken on the grill."

"Where did you learn to cook?"

We were walking to the kitchen.

"Not from Mother. Why do you think I was such a little fatso? From eating the junk she bought. Snacks, sodas, and pizza that tastes like cardboard. I have fat cells that will scream for the rest of my life because of Mother. I'll never forgive her."

"We need to talk about this afternoon, Lucy. If you hadn't come home when you did, the police would have been looking for you."

"I worked out for an hour and a half, then took a shower."

"You were gone four and half hours."

"I had groceries to buy and a few other errands."

"Why didn't you answer the car phone?"

"I assumed it was someone trying to reach you. Plus, I've never used a car phone. I'm not twelve years old, Aunt Kay."

"I know you're not. But you don't live here and have never driven here before. I was worried."

"I'm sorry," she said.

We ate by firelight, both of us sitting on the floor around the butler's table. I had turned off lamps. Flames jumped and shadows danced as if celebrating a magic moment in the lives of my niece and me.

"What do you want for Christmas?" I asked, reaching for my wine.

"Shooting lessons," she said.

Wild Rice Salad with Cashews

While staying with her Aunt Kay, Lucy works up her appetite by tapping into Kay's downtown office computer system to try to learn who has been accessing Kay's work computer. By the time her aunt gets home from a long day and evening, Lucy has prepared a feast of chicken breasts in marinated olive oil, garlic, and lemon juice ready for the grill, a chilled salad of wild rice with cashews, peppers, and sesame oil, and bread. "Where did you learn to cook?" Kay asks. "Not from Mother," Lucy replies.

6 ounces/170 grams wild rice

1½ pints/1 litre chicken stock

3 tablespoons olive oil

8 ounces/225 grams de-seeded and chopped red or green peppers

4 ounces/115 grams cashews, coarsely chopped

2 spring onions, sliced

Dressing:

3 tablespoons seasoned rice vinegar or apple cider vinegar

2 tablespoons olive oil

1 tablespoon sesame oil

1 clove garlic, finely chopped

¼ teaspoon salt

Pinch of freshly ground pepper

Lettuce leaves, for serving

1. In a strainer, rinse the wild rice under cool running water; drain well. Into a large saucepan, put the wild rice and chicken stock; bring to the boil over high heat. Reduce the heat and simmer, covered, for 45 to 50 minutes, until tender. Drain off any excess liquid; set aside.

2. Meanwhile, in a medium frying pan, heat the olive oil over medium-high heat; add the peppers and cook for 3 to 5 minutes, or until tender. Add the cashews and spring onions; cook for 2 to 3 minutes longer, or until the nuts begin to brown. Remove from the heat.

3. In a large bowl, toss together the wild rice and pepper mixture.

4. For the dressing: in a jar with a tight-fitting lid, combine the vinegar, olive and sesame oils, garlic, salt, and pepper. Cover and shake until blended; pour the dressing over the salad and toss until evenly coated. Cover and refrigerate salad for at least 2 hours or up to overnight to allow the flavours to blend.

5. To serve the salad, spoon it onto a lettuce-lined platter.

| MAKES 6 TO 8 SIDE-DISH SERVINGS |

Grilled Grouper with Butter and Key Lime Juice

The sea bass family of fish includes more than 300 species of small to large fish, including grouper. Also known as rock cod or jewfish, grouper thrives in the warm waters surrounding the reefs along the Atlantic coast from North Carolina to Florida, and along the Gulf and Mexican coasts as well. Favoured for its lean white meat and mildly sweet flavour, grouper is most often used in chowders or served as simply cooked fillets.

Both grouper and sea bass are great on the grill. Willie Travers, Jennifer Deighton's former husband, prepares fresh grouper for Kay in *Cruel & Unusual by marinating the fillets in Key lime juice, butter, and olive oil at his cottage in Fort Myers Beach. Then he grills the fish quickly and serves it with his Hearty Seven-Grain Bread (page 66), Marinated Coleslaw with Apple Cider Vinaigrette (page 69), and Dos Equis Mexican beer. Even Kay couldn't improve on that.*

SHORTCUT TIP: *If you don't have time to wait for 30 minutes of marinating, just 10 minutes will do.*

1¼ to 1½ pounds/565 to 675 grams grouper or sea bass fillets
(1 inch/2.5 centimetres thick)

2 ounces/55 grams butter, melted

4 tablespoons Key lime juice (see Note) or fresh lime juice

1 tablespoon olive oil

Finely grated zest of 1 lime

½ teaspoon salt

¼ teaspoon freshly ground pepper

Lime wedges, for serving

1 tablespoon chopped fresh chives

1. In a shallow glass or ceramic dish, place the fish fillets. Stir together the melted butter, lime juice, olive oil, lime zest, salt, and pepper; pour over the fish. Cover and refrigerate for 30 minutes.

2. Meanwhile, pre-heat the barbecue to medium-hot or pre-heat the grill. Remove the fish from the marinade and arrange the fillets on a lightly oiled grilling tray (or on the lightly oiled rack of the grill pan). Generously brush the fish with the marinade. Barbecue the fish for 9 to 12 minutes, until opaque throughout, turning the fish after 5 minutes and basting it several times with the butter mixture. (Or grill the fish 4 inches/10 centimetres from heat source for 6 to 8 minutes, turning after 3 minutes.)

3. To serve, arrange the fish and lime wedges on a platter and sprinkle the fish with the chives.

SERVES 4

NOTE: *See page 208 for a website address if you can't find Key lime juice in your local supermarket or speciality food shop.*

Hearty Seven-Grain Bread

This rustic bread is filled with high-fibre ingredients, whole grains, and honey for sweetness. Because of all the different grains used, this is a heavier bread that needs a longer time to rise to its full potential. Don't use a fast action yeast; give this dough the benefit of regular active dry yeast. Whole-grain flours, such as rye, contain less gluten, so do not let the dough rise until it's fully doubled in size, or it may collapse before baking. Let it rise three-quarters of the way towards doubling in size—that's enough.

No one sifts flour anymore, except flour for cakes, so there is no need to do that here. Check the temperature of the water with a thermometer, or test it on the inside of your wrist. If it feels very warm but not hot enough to be uncomfortable, it's ready to use.

Kay hardly ever uses butter—and prefers to serve bread brushed with or dipped in olive oil.

3 ounces/85 grams rye flour

2 ounces/55 grams finely chopped walnuts or pecans, toasted

2 ounces/55 grams rolled oats (old-fashioned or quick-cooking)

2 tablespoons sunflower seeds

2 tablespoons toasted wheatgerm

3 tablespoons sesame seeds, toasted if desired

15 to 18 ounces/425 to 510 grams bread or strong plain white flour

2 sachets dried yeast

1 tablespoon salt

14 fluid ounces/400 millilitres milk

4 tablespoons honey

2 ounces/55 grams butter

6 to 7 ounces/170 to 200 grams wholemeal flour

For Crust:

1 lightly beaten egg white

1 tablespoon water

Sesame seeds or sunflower seeds, for sprinkling

1. In a medium bowl, stir together the rye flour, nuts, oats, sunflower seeds, wheatgerm, and sesame seeds. Set aside.

2. In a large bowl, stir together 12½ ounces/355 grams of the bread flour, the yeast, and salt. In a medium saucepan, heat the milk, honey, and butter over medium heat, stirring, until it is very warm (120° to 130°F/48° to 54°C). Butter does not need to melt. Stir the milk mixture into the flour mixture, stirring until well combined. Stir in the rye-flour mixture until blended. Gradually stir in enough of the wholemeal flour to make a soft dough that leaves the side of the bowl.

3. Turn the dough out onto a generously floured surface and shape it into a ball. Knead the dough for about 10 minutes, until it is soft, smooth, and elastic, adding enough of the remaining bread flour to keep the dough from sticking. Place the dough into a greased bowl and turn to coat evenly. Cover the dough with a damp clean tea towel or cling film. Place the dough on the lowest oven rack. Turn the oven on to the lowest setting for 1 minute; then immediately turn the oven off. Let the dough rise for about 1 hour, until not quite doubled in size.

4. Punch down the dough; on a lightly floured surface, knead the dough 10 times to release the air bubbles. Cover and let rest for 10 minutes.

5. Shape the dough into loaves: cut the dough in half. Shape each half into a smooth, round ball. Place each ball on one large or two small greased baking sheets and flatten slightly with the palm of your hand.

6. In a small bowl, lightly beat the egg white and water; brush over the loaves. Sprinkle the loaves with the sesame or sunflower seeds. Cover the loaves and let rise 35 to 45 minutes, until not quite doubled in size.

7. Meanwhile, pre-heat the oven to 375°F/190°C/gas mark 5. Bake the loaves for 25 to 30 minutes, or until golden brown and they sound hollow when lightly tapped on the bottom. Transfer the loaves to a wire rack to cool slightly. Serve the bread warm or at room temperature with butter or olive oil.

| MAKES 2 LOAVES |

Marinated Coleslaw with Apple Cider Vinaigrette

There's nothing more all-American than coleslaw, and there are about as many variations of it as there are ethnic groups in America. Combining both red and green cabbage makes this version both colourful and appealing.

Apple cider vinegar, honey, and celery seed flavour the tangy vinaigrette dressing that is first boiled and then cooled. You might think that a marinated coleslaw like this one will become limp and uninteresting in the refrigerator. On the contrary, you will find that, like the live-wire guest who can always be relied upon to jazz up the party, this salad never fails to add a sure-shot of pizzazz to the menu.

SHORTCUT TIPS: *You can substitute 2 pounds/900 grams of store-bought coleslaw salad mix for the shredded cabbage and carrot. Also, you can halve the recipe to serve four.*

Dressing:

4 tablespoons cider vinegar

4 tablespoons olive oil

2 tablespoons honey

1/2 teaspoon celery seeds

1/2 teaspoon dry mustard

Salt and freshly ground pepper

Salad:

8 ounces/225 grams finely shredded green cabbage, plus leaves for garnish

8 ounces/225 grams finely shredded red cabbage

1 red or yellow pepper, de-seeded and thinly sliced

3 ounces/85 grams grated carrot

2 spring onions, thinly sliced

1. For the dressing: in a small saucepan, whisk together the vinegar, olive oil, honey, celery seeds, mustard, and salt and pepper to taste. Bring the mixture to the boil over medium-high heat; remove from the heat. Let the dressing cool for 15 minutes.

2. In a large bowl, toss together the green and red cabbage, pepper, carrot, and spring onions. Pour the dressing over and toss well. Cover and refrigerate the coleslaw for at least 4 hours or up to overnight to allow the flavours to blend.

3. To serve the coleslaw, line a serving bowl with cabbage leaves. Use a slotted spoon to spoon the coleslaw into the bowl.

SERVES 8

Kay's overall philosophy about the foods she uses in cooking is simple: use only the best ingredients. Kay knows that a murder case is only as good as the evidence that can be delivered; she knows equally well that both the final taste and the delectable appearance of the dishes she prepares depend almost entirely on the quality of the ingredients that go into them.

Good cooks, whether they spend a lot of time in the kitchen or not, depend on a well-stocked store-cupboard to save the day. Here's a representative list of most of the store-cupboard staples used in this book, items that you would find in Kay's store-cupboard, should you be lucky enough to visit. Together with the fresh cheeses, fruits, vegetables, meats, and seafood Kay keeps on hand in the refrigerator and her freezerful of sauces and pastas, she whips up her legendary gourmet meals.

Oils and Vinegars

- Extra-virgin olive oil
- Pure olive oil (for deep-frying)
- Truffle oil
- Non-stick cooking spray
- Mayonnaise or salad dressing
- Red and white wine vinegars
- Balsamic vinegar

Seasonings

- Jars of pre-chopped and crushed garlic
- Capers
- Dry mustard
- Ground nutmeg

- Saffron threads
- Salt
- Sesame seeds
- Bay leaves
- Black peppercorns and coarsely ground pepper
- White pepper

Stocks, Sauces, and Vegetables

- Low-fat beef, vegetable, and chicken stock (tinned or containers)
- Bottled barbecue sauce
- Bottled Italian dressing
- Tinned crushed tomatoes in purée
- Tinned diced tomatoes with Italian seasonings and with mild green chillies and onion
- Tomato purée
- Marinara sauce
- V-8 juice
- Clam juice
- Worcestershire sauce
- Spicy yellow mustard
- Tomato ketchup
- Tinned or bottled artichoke hearts or bottoms
- Onions

Baking Supplies

- Bread flour or strong plain white flour
- Wholemeal flour
- Rye flour

- Yellow cornmeal

- 5-minute or quick-cook polenta

- Cornflour

- Granola

- Honey

- Vanilla extract

- Sweetened condensed milk

- Dried figs, raisins

- Active dry yeast, both regular and fast action

- Baking soda or bicarbonate of soda, baking powder

- Sugars, granulated and soft light brown

- Sweet and unsweetened baking chocolate

- Chocolate chips

- Butterscotch, peanut butter, white chocolate chips

- Pine nuts

- Old-fashioned rolled oats

Miscellaneous

- A variety of good-quality dried pastas

- Bottled Key lime juice (see Note on page 65)

- Fresh breadcrumbs

- Wild rice

- Anchovies

- Several types of coffee beans

I got a taxi, and the driver, who was local and called himself Cowboy, told me he wrote songs and played piano when he wasn't in a cab. By the time he got me to the Hyatt, I knew he went to Chicago once a year to please his wife, and that he regularly drove ladies from Johnson City who came here to shop in the malls. I was reminded of the innocence people like me had lost, and I gave Cowboy an especially generous tip. He waited while I checked into my room, then took me to Calhoun's, which overlooked the Tennessee River and promised the best ribs in the USA.

The restaurant was extremely busy, and I had to wait at the bar. It was the University of Tennessee's homecoming weekend, I discovered, and everywhere I looked I found jackets and sweaters in flaming orange, and alumni of all ages drinking and laughing and obsessing about this afternoon's game. Their raucous instant replays rose from every corner, and if I did not focus on any one conversation, what I heard was a constant roar.

The Vols had beat the Gamecocks, and it had been a battle as serious as any fought in the history of the world. When men in UT hats on either side occasionally turned my way for agreement, I was very sincere in my nods and affirmations, for to admit in that room that I had not *been there* would surely come across as treason. I was not taken to my table until close to ten P.M., by which time my anxiety level was quite high.

I ate nothing Italian or sensible this night, for I had not eaten well in days and finally I was starving. I ordered baby back ribs, biscuits, and salad, and when the bottle of Tennessee Sunshine Hot Pepper Sauce said "Try Me," I did. Then I tried the Jack Daniel's pie. The meal was wonderful. Throughout it I sat beneath Tiffany lamps in a quiet corner looking out at the river. It was alive with lights reflected from the bridge in varying lengths and intensities, as if the water were measuring electronic levels for music I could not hear.

I tried not to think about crime.

Fruit-Marinated Lamb Kebabs

La Petite France at 2108 Maywill Street is one of my favourite restaurants in Richmond, where you can forget about life as you know it and let yourself be spoiled by Chef Paul Elbling and his wife, Marie-Antoinette. As Kay relates in The Body Farm, *"That night I took Lucy to La Petite France, where I surrendered to Chef Paul, who sentenced us to languid hours of Fruit-Marinated Lamb Kebabs and a bottle of 1986 Château Gruaud Larose."*

Marinate the lamb cubes the night before to let them soak up the spicy fruit flavours. Unless you have six very long barbecue skewers (12 to 14 inches/30 to 35 centimetres in length), you'll need a dozen metal skewers to spear all of the meat and vegetables. Serve the kebabs with an herbed rice pilaf or couscous. A Beaujolais, pinot noir, or red Bordeaux wine will also help you savour the lamb.

Fruit Marinade:

6 fluid ounces/170 millilitres apple juice

6 fluid ounces/170 millilitres pineapple juice

2 tablespoons fresh lime juice

2 cloves garlic, finely chopped

1 teaspoon salt

1/2 teaspoon ground allspice

1/2 teaspoon ground nutmeg

1/2 teaspoon ground cloves

1/4 teaspoon freshly ground pepper

Kebabs:

1¾ to 2-pounds/790 to 900 grams boneless leg of lamb, trimmed of
   fat and cut into 2-inch/5-centimetre cubes

12 medium mushrooms, trimmed

1 large onion, cut into 1½-inch/4-centimetre wedges

1 green pepper, de-seeded and cut into 1½-inch/4-centimetre squares

1 red pepper, de-seeded and cut into 1½-inch/4-centimetre squares

6 to 12 cherry tomatoes, for garnish

Hot cooked rice or couscous to serve

1. In a self-sealing plastic bag or shallow glass or ceramic dish, combine all the marinade ingredients until well blended. Set aside 4 tablespoons of the marinade. Add the lamb cubes to the marinade and turn the bag over several times to coat the meat all over (or toss the lamb in the dish). Refrigerate lamb (cover the dish, if used) for 8 to 12 hours or up to overnight, turning the bag over occasionally (or tossing the lamb in the dish occasionally).

2. To grill the kebabs: heat the barbecue to medium-hot or pre-heat the grill. Remove the lamb from the marinade and discard the marinade. On 6 long metal barbecue skewers, thread the lamb alternately with the mushrooms, onion wedges, and peppers, allowing a little bit of space between each item for even cooking. Arrange the skewers on a lightly oiled grilling tray or in the grill pan. Brush the skewers with some of the reserved marinade.

3. Barbecue the kebabs for about 8 minutes for medium-rare, turning the kebabs after 4 minutes and basting several times with reserved marinade. (Or grill 4 inches/10 centimetres from the heat source for 8 minutes for medium-rare.) Discard the remaining marinade.

4. To serve, place a cherry tomato on the end of each kebab. Pass the hot cooked rice or couscous separately.

SERVES 6

Zuppa di Aglio Fresco

(Fresh Garlic Soup)

*A*fter Lucy's hospital stay from a near-fatal car accident in The Body Farm, *her Aunt Kay brings her home for some R & R. Kay "put on a pot of* Zuppa di Aglio Fresco, *a fresh garlic soup popular in the hills of Brisighella, where it has been fed to babies and the elderly for many years."* This wonderful soup is the Italian version of chicken soup, a comforting potage of chicken stock, carrots, thyme, bay leaf, and sherry, thickened with egg yolks and enriched with Parmigiano-Reggiano. Kay serves the soup with Ravioli with Squash and Chestnut Filling (page 80).

The best way to peel and crush garlic is first to pull off the loose papery skin from the whole head, then separate the cloves. Place one or two cloves on a chopping board, and lay the flat side of a wide-bladed knife over them. Punch the flat of the knife with one strike of your fist, and voila! The husk falls away from the cloves and you have crushed garlic.

SHORTCUT TIP: *Look for jars of peeled whole garlic cloves in your super-market.*

4 tablespoons olive oil

9 ounces/255 grams finely chopped carrots

10 cloves garlic, peeled and crushed

32 fluid ounces/910 millilitres home-made chicken stock or ready-made chicken stock

1 tablespoon chopped fresh thyme

1 bay leaf

4 tablespoons dry sherry

3 very large egg yolks

2 ounces/55 grams freshly grated Parmigiano-Reggiano

2 tablespoons chopped fresh flat-leaf parsley

Salt and freshly ground pepper

4 slices (1-inch/2.5-centimetres thick) day-old sourdough, multi-grain,
   or country-style bread

1. In a large saucepan, heat 2 tablespoons of the olive oil; add the carrots and garlic. Cook over medium-high heat, stirring frequently, for 3 to 5 minutes, or until tender but not brown.

2. Stir in the chicken stock, thyme, and bay leaf. Bring the mixture to the boil over high heat. Reduce the heat to low and simmer, covered, for 30 minutes.

3. Discard the bay leaf. In a blender or food processor, purée the soup in several batches, transferring the purée to a large bowl. Return the puréed mixture to the rinsed-out saucepan; stir in the sherry.

4. In a small bowl, whisk together the egg yolks and the remaining 2 tablespoons oil; whisk in the Parmigiano-Reggiano until blended. Gradually whisk 4 tablespoons of the soup into the yolk mixture; whisk mixture into the soup. Heat the soup over medium-low heat, stirring constantly, for 8 to 10 minutes, until the soup thickens (do not boil or the soup will curdle). Stir in the parsley; season to taste with salt and freshly ground pepper. Remove the soup from the heat.

5. To serve the soup, place a slice of bread in each soup bowl. Ladle the soup over the bread and serve immediately.

SERVES 4

Ravioli with Squash and Chestnut filling

Legend has it that ravioli was first made aboard ships that left Genoa's port for long voyages, in an effort to make use of every bit of food that was brought on board. Bits of leftover meats and vegetables from one day's meal were chopped up, combined, and stuffed into pockets of pasta dough to be served the next day. Kay's ravioli features a squash and chestnut purée, a reflection of how far ravioli has come since its humble beginnings. (Look for tinned chestnut purée in the gourmet food sections of larger supermarkets or at Italian delis.)

Making ravioli is fun, because it's simple to do and it's easy to make a half dozen servings once you get the hang of it. Remember to start with rolled pasta that has dried for no more than 1 hour, because it needs to be moist enough to hold the filling securely. Picture dividing your sheets of dough into 1¹/₂-inch/4-centimetre squares when you spoon the mounds of filling onto the pasta. (Place a ruler just above your pasta sheet as an easy guide.) Each mound will be at the centre of the square, and you'll be cutting around each square to make the ravioli. A ravioli cutter, which has a rolling zigzag edge, will give that pinking-shear look to the edges of the pasta; a sharp knife can also be used.

A ravioli pan is a surefire way to make perfect squares of ravioli. You will have to roll and cut out pasta sheets that fit the pan exactly. Follow the manufacturer's directions for filling the ravioli.

If you have leftover cooked ravioli, you can enjoy it the next day: add it to 24 or 32 fluid ounces/680 or 910 millilitres of simmering chicken or vegetable stock. Cook just 1 or 2 minutes until heated through. Sprinkle with lots of grated Parmigiano-Reggiano and serve it with your favourite bread.

MAKE-AHEAD TIP: *You can freeze cooked and well-drained ravioli, layered flat between sheets of greaseproof paper, in a tightly covered freezer container, for up to a month.*

SHORTCUT TIP: *Instead of Kay's fresh pasta, you can use store-bought fresh pasta sheets.*

1 recipe Kay's Fresh Pasta (page 52) or store-bought fresh pasta sheets

1½ teaspoons olive oil

1½ ounces/45 grams finely chopped onion

8 ounces/225 grams mashed cooked squash such as butternut, acorn, or kabocha

2 ounces/55 grams tinned chestnut purée

1 very large egg

2 tablespoons honey

¼ teaspoon ground nutmeg

¼ teaspoon salt

1 recipe Béchamel Sauce (page 157)

Freshly grated Parmigiano-Reggiano, for sprinkling

Chopped fresh chives or fresh parsley, for garnish

1. Mix, knead, and let the pasta dough rest as directed To roll and cut the pasta: *if hand-rolling the pasta,* roll each piece of the dough into a 16x9-inch/41x23-centimetre rectangle. *If using the pasta-machine method,* roll the sheets about 4 inches/10 centimetres wide or a bit wider. Dry the rolled

pasta, uncovered, for 30 minutes. If pasta must be held longer, cover it well with cling film or clean tea towels for up to 1 hour.

2. While the pasta is drying, prepare the filling. In a small frying pan, heat the olive oil over medium heat. Add the onion and cook, stirring, for 3 to 5 minutes, until tender and golden brown.

3. In a blender or food processor, combine the squash, chestnut purée, and egg; blend the mixture until smooth. Add the onion mixture, honey, nutmeg, and salt; blend until puréed.

4. To cut and fill the ravioli: cut each sheet of pasta dough into 4-inch-/10-centimetre-wide rectangles (the length can vary, but trim the edges of each pasta sheet so they are straight). Place one pasta rectangle on a lightly floured chopping board. Keep the remaining dough covered. Drop mounds of the squash filling in 2 lengthwise rows, using a rounded teaspoonful for each mound, placing them 1$\frac{1}{2}$ inches/4 centimetres apart and leaving a $\frac{1}{2}$-inch/1.25-centimetre border on all sides.

5. Brush the dough around the filling and along the edges with water (this will help the dough seal when the ravioli are cut).

6. Drape a second sheet of pasta on top, carefully pressing around each mound of filling to seal the two sheets and to create ravioli squares. If the bottom rectangle is longer or shorter than the top one, cut the top rectangle at a point half-way between two mounds of filling, then fill in with another rectangle to cover the remaining mounds of filling. Seal the dough all around with wet fingers, pressing the pasta around each mound of filling and along edges to secure.

7. Using a sharp knife, a pizza cutter, or a ravioli cutter, cut the ravioli into squares by cutting lengthwise between the 2 rows of mounds, then cutting crosswise between each pair of mounds. (Makes 54 to 60 ravioli.)

8. To cook the ravioli: in a large pan, bring 6$\frac{1}{2}$ pints/4 litres of salted water to the boil. Add the ravioli, about 10 at a time, by sliding them off a large spoon or spatula into the boiling water. Reduce the heat to a gentle boil,

stirring occasionally to keep ravioli separated. Cook the ravioli for about 3 minutes, or until *al dente* (tender but still firm to the bite). Drain on a kitchen paper-lined plate.

9. Serve the hot ravioli topped with the béchamel sauce, grated Parmigiano-Reggiano, and chives or parsley.

SERVES 6 TO 7

(8 TO 9 RAVIOLI PER PERSON)

Barbecued Baby Back Ribs

C alhoun's Restaurant in West Knoxville, located at 400 Neyland Drive, overlooks the Tennessee River on the University of Tennessee campus. In The Body Farm, *Kay dines at the restaurant while staying in Knoxville to gather evidence about the Temple Gault murders. A fixture since the early 1980s, Calhoun's is known for their award-winning "best ribs in America," and they certainly have the "taste of Tennessee" down pat.*

Here they share their recipe for their pride and joy, baby back pork ribs, smoked with Tennessee hickory and slathered with their signature Bar-B-Que Sauce. The barbecue sauce, which boasts 20 secret ingredients, comes from an age-old Smoky Mountain recipe. You can order it directly from the restaurant's website, www.calhouns.com. For a smoky Tennessee flavour, add some pre-soaked hickory chips to your coals. One slab (1 pound/450 grams) of ribs is about right for a hearty serving, since the ribs themselves do not have a lot of meat on them. Guests with smaller appetites will be satisfied with a half slab (8 ounces/225 grams) of the ribs.

Follow Kay's lead and round out your meal with some hot biscuits, tossed salad, and very cold beer, or a dry chardonnay, sauvignon blanc, or a light red wine.

1¾ pints/970 millilitres water

1 tablespoon liquid smoke (see Note on page 85)

1½ teaspoons salt

½ teaspoon garlic powder

¼ teaspoon ground white pepper

4 slabs baby back pork ribs (4 pounds/2 kilograms)

12 fluid ounces/340 millilitres Calhoun's BBQ Sauce or other barbecue sauce

1. Pre-heat the oven to 275°F/140°C/gas mark 1. In a large shallow roasting tin, stir together 32 fluid ounces/910 millilitres of the water and the liquid smoke. It should come ½ inch/1.25 centimetres up the sides of the tin; add more water, if necessary.

2. In a small bowl, stir together the salt, garlic powder, and white pepper. Sprinkle the mixture evenly over the meaty side of the ribs. Place the ribs, meat side up, in the roasting tin. Cover the tin tightly with aluminium foil.

3. Bake the ribs for 2 hours and 15 minutes. Remove the ribs from the oven and let stand, covered, for 15 minutes.

4. To grill: pre-heat the barbecue to medium or pre-heat the grill. In a 1½-pint/1-litre saucepan, combine the barbecue sauce and the remaining water. (This helps prevent the sauce from burning on the grill.) Heat the mixture just until it simmers; remove from the heat. Arrange the ribs on the hot grill (or on the rack in a grill pan). Cook for 10 to 12 minutes, turning and basting with the barbecue sauce mixture every 2 minutes, being careful not to allow the sauce to burn. (Or grill the ribs for 8 to 10 minutes, turning and basting every 2 minutes.)

5. To serve, baste the ribs with the barbecue sauce; cut the racks between the bones into 2-rib portions.

SERVES 4 TO 6

NOTE: *Liquid smoke is an American food flavouring made from the smoke of burning hickory and other smoke-house woods. It gives food a smoked flavour and can be bought on the Internet from American stockists.*

Jack Daniel's Chocolate-Pecan Pie

O
n the tail end of Calhoun's mouth-watering menu of barbecue special-ities are the inevitable desserts. If you've ever played the dinner party game of planning the last menu of your life, here's a to-die-for pudding you will want to consider. This unbelievably delicious pecan pie is studded throughout with chocolate and laced with Tennessee whiskey. Serve it warm, cut into modest-sized pieces, and savour every bite. After that, there's no place to go but straight to heaven.

MAKE-AHEAD TIP: If you are preparing the pie a day ahead, cool the pie on a rack for 1 hour after baking, then cover and refrigerate. For the best flavour, let the refrigerated pie stand at room temperature for 1 hour before serving.

SHORTCUT TIP: If you don't have time to make the pastry, use store-bought refrigerated or frozen (defrosted) sweet/dessert shortcrust pastry. Just roll out one of the pieces of pastry, place into a pie tin, trim, and flute the edge as directed in step 1.

12–14 ounces/340–400 grams sweet/dessert shortcrust pastry dough
for one 9-inch/23-centimetre pie

3 very large eggs

2 very large egg yolks

4 ounces/115 grams sugar

6 fluid ounces/170 millilitres dark corn syrup (see Note on page 87)

2½ ounces/70 grams butter, melted

4 tablespoons Jack Daniel's or whiskey

4 ounces/115 grams chopped bittersweet chocolate or semi-sweet
chocolate chips

6 ounces/170 grams pecan halves or pieces

Vanilla ice cream, for serving

1. Pre-heat the oven to 350°F/180°C/gas mark 4. Roll out the pastry on a lightly floured surface, then ease the pastry dough into a deep 9-inch/23-centimetre pie tin. Trim and flute the edge of the dough, if desired, or trim the dough even with the edge of the tin. Place the pie tin on a baking sheet.

2. In a large bowl, whisk together the eggs, egg yolks, and sugar until well combined. Whisk in the corn syrup, melted butter, and Jack Daniel's until well blended.

3. Sprinkle 2 ounces/55 grams of the chocolate chips over the bottom of the pastry crust. Pour in the pie filling. Sprinkle 2 ounces/55 grams of the pecans over the filling. Sprinkle the remaining chocolate chips over, then top with the remaining 4 ounces/115 grams pecans.

4. Bake the pie for 50 to 55 minutes, or until set in the centre. Turn off the oven; leave the pie in the oven, with the door closed, for 15 minutes longer to crisp the top. Transfer the pie to a wire rack to cool for at least 2 hours. To serve, cut into small wedges and top with vanilla ice cream.

MAKES ONE 9-INCH/23-CENTIMETRE PIE

NOTE: *Corn syrup gives the best results when making this recipe – golden syrup is not a good substitute. Corn syrup can be brought from specialist American food shops.*

round the corner of the Museum of Natural History was the snowcapped pink awning of a restaurant called Scaletta, which I was surprised to find lit up and noisy. A couple in fur coats turned in and went downstairs, and I wondered if we shouldn't do the same. I was actually getting hungry, and Wesley didn't need to lose any more weight.

"Are you up for this?" I asked him.

"Absolutely. Is Scaletta a relative of yours?" he teased.

"I think not."

We got as far as the door, where the maître d' informed us that the restaurant was closed.

"You certainly don't look closed," I said, suddenly exhausted and unwilling to walk any more.

"But we are, signora." He was short, balding and wearing a tuxedo with a bright red cummerbund. "This is a private party."

"Who is Scaletta?" Wesley asked him.

"Why do you want to know?"

"It is an interesting name, much like mine," I said.

"And what is yours?"

"Scarpetta."

He looked carefully at Wesley and seemed puzzled. "Yes, of course. But he is not with you this evening?"

I stared blankly at him. "Who is not with me?"

"Signor Scarpetta. He was invited. I'm sorry, I did not realize you were in his party…"

"Invited to what?" I had no idea what he was talking about. My name was rare.

I had never encountered another Scarpetta, not even in Italy.

The maître d' hesitated. "You are not related to Scarpetta who comes here often?"

"What Scarpetta?" I said, getting uneasy.

"A man. He has been here many times recently. A very good customer. He was invited to our Christmas party. So you are not his guests?"

"Tell me more about him," I said.

"A young man. He spends much money." The maître d' smiled.

I could feel Wesley's interest pique. He said, "Can you describe him?"

"I have many people inside. We reopen tomorrow…"

Wesley discreetly displayed his shield. The man regarded it calmly.

"Of course." He was polite but unafraid. "I find you a table.'

"No, no," Wesley said. "You don't have to do that. But we need to ask more about this man who said his last name was Scarpetta."

"Come in." He motioned us. "We talk, we may as well sit. You sit, you may as well eat. My name is Eugenio."

He led us to a pink-covered table in a corner far removed from guests in party clothes filling most of the dining room.

They were toasting, eating, talking and laughing with the gestures and cadences of Italians.

"We do not have full menu tonight," Eugenio apologized. "I can bring you *costoletta di vitello alla griglia* or *pollo al limone* with maybe a little *capellini primavera* or *rigatoni con broccolo*."

We said yes to all and added a bottle of Dolcetto D'Alba, which was a favorite of mine and difficult to find.

Shrimp Sauté
with Garlic and Lemon

Kay is invited to dinner at NYPD Commander Frances Penn's light, bright fifteenth-floor apartment on the West Side of Manhattan, to discuss the Temple Gault murder case. The Commander's menu is simple but elegant: sautéed shrimps, warm bread, and steamed asparagus, served with a crisp chardonnay. It takes as little as 10 minutes to marinate the shrimps, for a zing of lemon-garlic flavour.

To steam asparagus, snap off the bottom woody portions of the stalks. Arrange the spears in a steamer basket set over a pan of simmering water. Cook the asparagus, partially covered, for 4 to 8 minutes (depending on the thickness of the stalks) until they are nearly tender. Drizzle the asparagus with a bit of extra-virgin olive oil and season with salt and pepper. Add a healthy grating of Parmigiano-Reggiano or a sprinkling of your favourite chopped fresh herbs.

Marinade:

2 tablespoons olive oil

2 tablespoons fresh lemon juice

2 cloves garlic, finely chopped

12 ounces/340 grams jumbo shrimps (about 10 to 12 shrimps), peeled and de-veined

Sauté:

2 tablespoons olive oil

½ ounce/15 grams butter

2 shallots, chopped

2 large cloves garlic, slivered

1 tablespoon fresh lemon juice

2 tablespoons chopped fresh parsley

Salt and freshly ground pepper

Lemon wedges, for serving

1. For the marinade: in a medium non-metallic bowl, combine the oil, lemon juice, and garlic. Add the shrimps, turning to coat with the marinade. Cover and refrigerate for 10 to 30 minutes.

2. With a slotted spoon, remove the shrimps from the marinade; discard the marinade. In a medium frying pan, heat the olive oil with the butter over medium-high heat. Add the shrimps and cook, stirring and turning the shrimps frequently, for 2 to 3 minutes, until they just turn pink and opaque throughout. Immediately remove the shrimps from the pan; set aside.

3. In the same pan, add the shallots and garlic. Cook over medium-high heat, stirring frequently, for 3 minutes. Stir in the lemon juice and parsley. Return the shrimps to the pan and cook for 1 minute longer, or until heated through. Season with salt and pepper. Serve immediately with lemon wedges.

SERVES 2

Funghi e Carciofi

(Mushroom and Artichoke Starter)

This unusual starter from Scaletta's Restaurant in New York is worth going off your low-fat diet for one evening. After all, you'll be using olive oil for the frying, which has no cholesterol, and there is no breading on the artichokes and mushrooms. Share this simple starter with five friends, so you'll have just a modest portion to indulge in.

Make certain that your vegetables have been patted dry with kitchen paper to avoid excess spattering during frying.

In From Potter's Field, *Temple Gault* enjoys this dish with a couple of French white wines, such as Château Carbonnieux and Château Olivier. Other appropriate choices would be a crisp California chardonnay, an Italian pinot grigio, or a light red, such as Bordeaux or rosé.

24 medium mushrooms (10 to 12 ounces/280 to 340 grams)

14 ounces/400 grams tinned or bottled artichoke bottoms or hearts, drained

16 fluid ounces/455 millilitres olive oil

5 to 6 cloves garlic, crushed

3 tablespoons chopped fresh basil, plus leaves for garnish

Salt and freshly ground pepper

Freshly grated Parmigiano-Reggiano, for sprinkling

1. Cut off the stems from the mushrooms. Cut the mushroom caps into quarters or thirds. Pat the artichoke bottoms (or hearts) dry with kitchen paper; cut into quarters (or use hearts as is).

2. In a deep frying pan or large saucepan, heat the olive oil with the garlic until the oil reaches 375°F/190°C on a deep-fry thermometer. Remove the garlic with a slotted spoon. (Otherwise, the garlic will burn and impart an unpleasant flavour to your vegetables.) Using the slotted spoon, add the mushroom and artichoke pieces, a few at a time, to the hot oil. Cook for 3 to 4 minutes, or until the vegetables are golden brown.

3. Transfer the vegetables to kitchen paper to drain well. Wait 1 to 2 minutes between cooking each batch to allow the oil to return to the proper temperature.

4. Toss the hot vegetables with the chopped basil and season with salt and pepper. Cool for 2 to 3 minutes. To serve, transfer the hot vegetables to small plates. Sprinkle with Parmigiano-Reggiano and serve immediately garnished with basil leaves.

MAKES 4 TO 6 STARTER
OR FIRST-COURSE SERVINGS

Pollo al Limone

(Lemon Chicken)

t's Christmas, and Kay and Benton Wesley have spent the day in New York City, retracing serial killer Temple Gault's steps in the neighbourhood of Central Park West and 81st Street, where he had been spotted in the subway station with his latest victim. Kay is attracted to the pink awning of a restaurant called Scaletta's, where she and Benton have an illuminating discussion with Eugenio, the maître d'. It seems that Gault has practically become a regular at the restaurant in recent days, helping himself to several of their best entrées and white wines, on Kay's stolen American Express Gold card.

I discovered Scaletta's quite by accident. While researching the New York subway system for the book, I came out of the subway one day at the Museum of Natural History and around the corner I saw Scaletta's at 50 West 77th Street. I thought how remarkable it was that its name was so close to Scarpetta. Since then I've dined there several times and am a real fan of Chef Omer Grgurev.

Pollo al Limone is one of the dishes that Eugenio presents to Kay and Benton, along with Rigatoni con Broccolo (page 129). A bottle of Dolcetto D'Alba, 1979, a favourite of Kay's, is their wine of choice this evening. It's very light, like a Beaujolais.

SHORTCUT TIP: In place of the clarified butter, you can use equal parts of extra-virgin olive oil and regular butter. The oil keeps the butter from burning, and you will still get plenty of butter flavour.

6 skinless, boneless chicken breasts (2 pounds/900 grams total)

3 ounces/85 grams plain flour

½ teaspoon salt

¼ teaspoon freshly ground pepper

3 tablespoons clarified butter (see Note)

Sauce:

12 fluid ounces/340 millilitres home-made chicken stock or ready-
made chicken stock

4 fluid ounces/115millilitres dry white wine

4 tablespoons fresh lemon juice

½ teaspoon salt

⅛ teaspoon ground white pepper

3 tablespoons chopped fresh parsley

Lemon slices, for garnish

Hot cooked pasta

1. Place one chicken breast between two pieces of greaseproof paper or inside a self-sealing plastic bag. Pound the chicken with a meat mallet to ¼-inch/6 millimetres thickness. Repeat with the remaining chicken. In a small bowl, stir together the flour, salt, and pepper. Coat the chicken with the seasoned flour, shaking off the excess. Arrange the chicken on a greaseproof paper-lined baking sheet or tray.

2. Pour 2 tablespoons of the clarified butter into a large frying pan. Brown the chicken over medium-high heat for about 3 minutes per side. Transfer the chicken to a plate and set aside. Wipe out the pan with kitchen paper.

3. To make the sauce: in the same pan, combine the chicken stock, white wine, lemon juice, salt, and white pepper. Bring to the boil over medium-high heat; reduce the heat to low and simmer, uncovered, for 5 to 8 minutes, or until the sauce is reduced by half.

4. Return the chicken pieces to the frying pan and spoon the sauce over the chicken. Cover and cook over medium heat for 2 to 3 minutes longer, or until the thickest part of the chicken is no longer pink. Uncover and add the remaining 1 tablespoon clarified butter to the pan. Simmer for 5 minutes longer, stirring frequently.

5. To serve, place a chicken breast on each plate. Stir the parsley into the sauce and spoon it over the chicken. Garnish with the lemon slices, and serve with the hot pasta.

| SERVES 6 |

NOTE: *To make clarified butter: start with cut up unsalted butter. Melt it completely over low heat in a small heavy-based saucepan without stirring it. Carefully pour the clear yellow liquid that is on top into a container. Discard the milky layer. You can refrigerate or freeze clarified butter, although it tends to become grainy when it solidifies. Use it only for browning or sautéing.*

PAGE 176

Bev's Lump Crab Cakes

(PRECEDING PAGE) PAGE 64

Grilled Grouper with
Butter and Key Lime Juice

PAGE 94

Pollo al Limone (Lemon Chicken)

PAGE 86

Jack Daniel's Chocolate-Pecan Pie

PAGE 44

Veal Breast Stuffed with Spinach Piston

Lasagne with Marinara Sauce
and Porcini Mushrooms

Greek Salad with Red Wine Vinaigrette

107

PAGE 50

Le Pappardelle del Cantunzein

(Yellow and Green Broad Noodles with Sweet Peppers and Sausage)

PAGE 84

Barbecued Baby Back Ribs

PAGE 62

Wild Rice Salad with Cashews

PAGE 76

Fruit-Marinated Lamb Kabobs

PAGE 154

Lasagne coi Carciofi

(Lasagne with Artichokes and Béchamel Sauce)

PAGE 178

Lila's Clam Stew

PAGE 152

Braided Country Bread

114

PAGE 174

Jumbo Shrimp with Bev's Kicked by a Horse
Cocktail Sauce

PAGE 42

New York Steaks with Red Wine Marinade

PAGE 164

Classic English Breakfast

(Bacon and Eggs with Tomatoes and Mushrooms)

PAGE 38

Omelet with Sweet Peppers and Onions

PAGE 182

Marino's Breakfast Bagel Sandwich

PAGE 129

Rigatoni con Broccolo
(Rigatoni with Broccoli)

PAGE 90

Shrimp Sauté with Garlic and Lemon

PAGE 184

Grilled Chicken Caesar Salad

PAGE 208

Key Lime Meringue Pie

PAGE 80

Ravioli with Squash and Chestnut Filling

126

PAGE 160

Fig, Melon, and Prosciutto Salad

(OVERLEAF) PAGE 139

Linguine with Olive Oil Parmesan, and Onion

127

Rigatoni con Broccolo

(Rigatoni with Broccoli)

Chef Omer at Scaletta's Restaurant in New York likes to use sliced garlic in this rigatoni side dish. Cutting the slices into slivers spreads the flavour even further. Extra-virgin olive oil is a must for this dish.

A safety note: remove the frying pan from the heat before pouring the wine into the pan. Otherwise, you might have a small bonfire on your hands.

MAKE-AHEAD TIP: *You can cook the broccoli and prepare the white sauce ahead of time and refrigerate them. Then you can easily whip up the broccoli sauce while the pasta is cooking.*

1 ½ pounds/675 grams broccoli

1 pound/450 grams rigatoni

2 tablespoons extra-virgin olive oil

4 cloves garlic, slivered

2 fluid ounces/55 milliltres dry white wine

8 fluid ounces/225 millilitres home-made chicken or veal stock or ready-
made chicken stock

2 fluid ounces/55 millilitres Omer's White Sauce (page 130)

1 teaspoon butter

½ teaspoon salt

¼ teaspoon freshly ground pepper

1 ½ ounces/45 grams freshly grated Parmigiano-Reggiano, plus additional
for serving

1. Trim the stems from the broccoli and cut it into small florets. Fill a large bowl with iced water. In a large saucepan, bring 6½ pints/4 litres of salted water to the boil. Add the broccoli and boil for 2 minutes, just to bring up the colour. Drain the broccoli and transfer to the bowl of iced water to stop the cooking. Pour off any water remaining in the pan.

2. In the same pan, bring 6½ pints/4 litres of fresh salted water to the boil. Cook the rigatoni according to the package directions until *al dente* (tender but still firm to the bite). Drain the pasta well and toss it with 1 tablespoon olive oil; set aside.

3. To make the sauce: in a large frying pan, heat the remaining oil over medium heat. Cook the garlic for 3 to 5 minutes until golden brown, being careful not to let it burn. Remove from the heat.

4. Add the white wine to the frying pan, then stir in the chicken stock. Return the pan to the heat and whisk in the white sauce. Bring the mixture to the boil over medium-high heat, stirring frequently. Reduce the heat to low and simmer for about 7 minutes, or until it is reduced by half.

5. Stir in the butter, salt, and pepper. Add the broccoli; simmer the mixture for 1 to 2 minutes longer, or until the broccoli is heated through.

6. Return the pasta to the pasta pan; add the broccoli sauce mixture and the Parmigiano-Reggiano; toss to coat well. Serve with extra Parmigiano-Reggiano alongside.

| MAKES 6 TO 8 SIDE-DISH SERVINGS |

Omer's White Sauce

SHORTCUT TIP: *This recipe yields enough sauce for four batches of Rigatoni con Broccolo. Freeze it in 1 tablespoonfuls by spooning the finished sauce into large ice cube trays. When frozen, pop out the cubes and freeze them in a self-sealing freezer bag. You'll have white sauce on hand any time you need it.*

2 tablespoons butter

2 tablespoons plain flour

4 fluid ounces/115 millilitres milk

4 fluid ounces/115 millilitres home-made chicken or veal stock or

    ready-made chicken stock

1/4 teaspoon salt

Pinch of freshly ground pepper

In a 1½-pint/1-litre saucepan, melt the butter over medium heat. Stir in the flour until blended. Add the milk and chicken stock all at once, stirring constantly, until the mixture thickens and bubbles. Cook, stirring, for 2 minutes longer. Stir in the salt and pepper. Makes 8 fluid ounces/225 millilitres of sauce.

Among the array of aromatic ingredients that Italian cooks have to choose from, the venerable garlic holds top culinary status. Its strong, unmistakable aroma and flavour come packaged in a plain papery skin that belies the versatility within.

Chopped into a vegetable sauté, crushed and rubbed over a lamb roast, sliced and stuffed under the skin of a chicken, finely chopped into a vinaigrette, or baked and spread over crusty bread, no other seasoning can hold a candle to the tantalizing flavour of garlic.

It's interesting to note that although garlic is such an important ingredient today in Italian cooking, it was once snubbed by wealthy Romans, who gave it to their slaves and labourers to give them strength. A veteran of 5,000 years of intriguing history, during which it was used largely for medicinal purposes, garlic has only been welcome in the kitchen for the past couple of hundred years.

Today, this member of the onion family and botanical cousin of the lily is plentiful in markets year-round.

Cooking with Garlic

Kay, the purist, prefers to begin with fresh garlic for all of her recipes. In a pinch, however, pre-chopped garlic and even jarred peeled fresh garlic cloves make handy substitutes that compromise the flavour only a little while saving on preparation time. When buying fresh garlic, look for well-shaped bulbs with papery skin, without soft or dented spots or green sprouts. If purchasing processed garlic, check the expiry date on the label.

Fresh garlic has a stronger, more pungent flavour than cooked garlic. When sautéing or browning garlic, take care not to let it burn; cook it just until golden. Burned garlic imparts an off-flavour to food and makes it taste bitter. Stews and soups containing garlic get the benefit of a sweeter garlic flavour because of the longer cooking at moderate to low temperatures. Baking or roasting garlic also softens or sweetens the flavour, because some of the pungent oils are released during cooking. It also softens the texture of garlic, which morphs into a spread with the consistency of thick mayonnaise. That's why roasted cloves of garlic are so coveted as a spread for bread.

Here are some tips on preparing fresh garlic:

PEELING AND CRUSHING GARLIC. You can use a garlic peeler, a gadget available in speciality kitchen shops, or use the fist-and-knife method: place a garlic clove on a chopping board, and lay the flat side of a large, preferably heavy knife over it. Hit the side of the knife once with your fist, and the paper husk will fall away, leaving a crushed clove of garlic.

CHOPPED GARLIC. For more than a few cloves of garlic, store-bought pre-peeled garlic is handy to start with. Or, peel the cloves, place them in a mini-food processor, and chop or mince as needed. For one or two cloves of garlic, see the instructions above for peeling garlic; then remove the peel and chop the crushed garlic.

MINCED GARLIC. This is very finely chopped garlic; simply cut a peeled clove of garlic one way, then slice again the other way into very small pieces.

CRUSHED GARLIC. When garlic is required to be very smooth for a recipe, crushed garlic may be needed. The best technique is to use a garlic press, although there may be a little waste, because a small portion of the clove may be left behind in the press.

Storage Tips

Store fresh garlic or garlic braids at room temperature, out of bright light or sunlight. Keep the bulbs or unpeeled cloves in open containers; never store a garlic bulb in a plastic produce bag—it needs good ventilation. Also, do not refrigerate garlic unless it has been peeled, because it needs to be kept dry. Properly stored, a garlic bulb should last about two months.

French Onion Soup

Kay, Marino, Lucy, and Lucy's companion and FBI cohort, Janet, leave the Quantico Marine Corps Base together and head for the Globe & Laurel at 18418 Jefferson Davis Highway in Triangle, VA for dinner and, of course, some serious conversation. A fixture in the area since 1968, the restaurant is dedicated to the proud history and traditions of the Marine Corps. Amidst the resplendent Highland plaid décor, police shoulder patches donated by the many law enforcement officers who frequent the Globe & Laurel are displayed. The restaurant's patch collection, which represents a number of foreign countries, is thought to be one of the world's largest.

Marine Major Richard T. Spooner, proprietor, has shared his rich, traditional French Onion Soup recipe—perfected over the past thirty years—with countless Marine Corps families, but this is the first time it has appeared in print. Spooner is adamant about using authentic sherry in this soup, in place of often poor-quality cooking sherry. And provolone cheese is his first choice for melting over the soup. "We have tried other cheeses, but find that provolone brings far more compliments," says Spooner. "Serve it with pride."

1½ tablespoons butter

1½ pounds/675 grams sliced onions (3 to 4 medium)

1 tablespoon plain flour

32 fluid ounces/910 millilitres home-made beef stock or ready-made beef stock

32 fluid ounces/910 millilitres home-made chicken stock or ready-made chicken stock

2 fluid ounces/55 millilitres dry sherry

2 medium tomatoes, peeled, de-seeded, if desired (see Note), and chopped

1 to 1½ teaspoons salt

¼ teaspoon freshly ground pepper

1 tablespoon beef gravy granules (optional)

8 slices (½-inch/1.25-centimetres thick) French or sourdough bread, lightly toasted

8 thin slices provolone cheese or other good melting cheese (about 6 ounces/170 grams)

1. In a flameproof casserole dish or large saucepan, melt the butter over medium-low heat. Add the onions and cook slowly for about 10 minutes, stirring frequently, until the onions begin to turn translucent and a nice golden colour.

2. Sprinkle the flour over the onions; cook, stirring with a wooden spoon, for 2 to 3 minutes longer. Stir in the beef stock, chicken stock, and sherry, then add the tomatoes. Bring the soup to the boil over medium-high heat. Reduce the heat and simmer, uncovered, for 15 minutes.

3. Stir in the salt and pepper (use the lower amount of salt if you plan to add the beef gravy granules). Add the beef gravy granules to yield a deeper colour and a stronger flavour, if desired. At this point, the soup is ready.

4. To serve, pre-heat the grill. Ladle the soup into a 5-pint/3-litre ovenproof casserole dish or 8 ovenproof bowls (put the casserole or bowls onto a sturdy rimmed baking tray for easier handling). Float the toasted bread slices in the soup and top with the cheese. Place the soup about 3 inches/8 centimetres from the heat source and grill just about 1 minute, until the cheese melts and browns slightly. Serve immediately.

SERVES 8

NOTE: *To peel and seed tomatoes: cut an "x" in the bottom of each tomato. Plunge the tomatoes into boiling water for 60 seconds; with a slotted spoon, transfer to a bowl of iced water for 2 minutes. Peel off the skins. Halve the tomatoes and squeeze out the seeds and juice.*

Tortellini Verdi

(Spinach Tortellini)

Benton Wesley drops Kay off at her home and orders her to barricade herself inside with Marino, Lucy, and Janet. After a traumatic day that included seeing a horrifying videotape of Temple Gault's latest murder, both Benton and Marino are concerned for Kay's safety. As Marino prepares Lucy and Janet for the worst, Kay rallies herself by trying to do something normal—and for her that means cooking. She checks the refrigerator for dinner prospects, trying to ignore the around-the-clock surveillance outside her home.

Tortellini look like funny little Italian hats, perhaps something that a bishop would wear, and they are usually stuffed with cheese or meat fillings. These satisfying little pastas make wonderful comfort food and, with a little time and patience, are easy to make from Kay's Fresh Spinach Pasta recipe. Kay keeps cooked tortellini on hand in her freezer for quick meals.

Only just-made pasta sheets, dried for 30 minutes, are moist enough to be filled and shaped for tortellini. Once shaped, they are ready to cook. Simmer them gently to keep their shape. Tortellini usually float up to the top of the pasta water when they are done.

MAKE-AHEAD TIP: You can refrigerate the cooked tortellini for up to several days, or freeze them on layers of greaseproof paper or aluminium foil in freezer containers for up to several months.

½ recipe Kay's Fresh Spinach Pasta (page 55)

Filling:

8 ounces/225 grams ricotta cheese

4 ounces/115 grams grated mozzarella cheese

1 ounce/25 grams freshly grated Parmigiano-Reggiano, plus additional
    for serving

2 tablespoons finely chopped fresh basil or oregano

1 tablespoon finely chopped fresh chives

1 egg white, lightly beaten

Sauce:

16 fluid ounces/455 millilitres Kay's Marinara Sauce (page 150) or
    other prepared marinara sauce

1. Make the pasta dough and roll out the pasta sheets as directed. While the pasta is drying, prepare the tortellini filling. In a bowl, stir together the ricotta, mozzarella, Parmigiano-Reggiano, basil or oregano, chives, and egg white until blended.

2. To make the tortellini: use a 2-inch/5-centimetre round cookie or biscuit cutter to cut out as many rounds as possible from the sheets of pasta dough. Discard the dough trimmings.

3. To stuff and shape the tortellini: place ½ teaspoon of the cheese filling in the centre of one round of dough. With your fingers, moisten the bottom edge of the round with water. Fold the circle in half, away from you, pressing the edges together with your fingers to seal tightly. Moisten the corners of the half-circle with water and bring them together towards you, overlapping them and pressing the ends together to seal. (The pasta dough and the filling make 65 to 70 tortellini.)

4. Place the filled and shaped tortellini on a greaseproof paper-lined baking sheet; keep covered with cling film until all of the tortellini are made.

5. To cook the tortellini: in a large pan, bring 6½ pints/4 litres of salted water to the boil. Add the tortellini in batches and cook, stirring occasionally, for about 5 minutes, or until *al dente* (tender but still firm to the bite). Drain well, but do not rinse.

6. Serve the tortellini topped with the marinara sauce and sprinkled with Parmigiano-Reggiano.

MAKES 8 FIRST-COURSE SERVINGS
OR 4 MAIN-DISH SERVINGS

Linguine with Olive Oil, Parmesan and Onion

Cooking for others is one way Kay expresses herself emotionally, and one of her favourite comfort foods is pasta. Preparing this simple, delicious pasta dish laced with olive oil (Kay favours extra-virgin), sautéed onions, and freshly grated Parmigiano-Reggiano, helps Kay feel she is comforting herself and those she loves. This is an excellent side dish served with grilled meat, fish, or poultry; or serve it as an entrée, lavished with the cheese.

1 recipe Kay's Fresh Pasta (page 52) cut into fettuccine (¼-inch-/ 6-millimetre-wide strips), or 2 packages (9 ounces/255 grams each) store-bought fresh fettuccine

4 to 5 tablespoons extra-virgin olive oil

6 ounces/170 grams chopped onions

½ tablespoon chopped fresh parsley

2 tablespoons chopped fresh basil

2 tablespoons chopped fresh thyme

1 tablespoon chopped fresh oregano

Salt and freshly ground pepper

2 ounces/55 grams freshly grated Parmigiano-Reggiano, plus additional for serving

1. If preparing Kay's Fresh Pasta: roll out the pasta and dry as directed, then

cut into fettuccine noodles or linguine noodles. Dry the noodles as directed in the recipe. In a large pan, bring 6½ pints/4 litres salted water and 1 tablespoon of the olive oil to the boil.

2. Meanwhile, in a small frying pan, heat 1 tablespoon of the olive oil over medium-low heat. Add the onions and cook, stirring frequently, for about 10 minutes until translucent and tender. Stir in the parsley, basil, thyme, and oregano. Remove from the heat and keep warm.

3. Cook the fettuccine in the boiling water for 2 to 5 minutes, until *al dente* (tender but still firm to the bite). Immediately drain well. Do not rinse. (Cook store-bought fettuccine according to the package directions.)

4. Turn the pasta into a large serving bowl. Add the onion-herb mixture and season with salt and pepper. Drizzle generously with the remaining olive oil, sprinkle with 2 ounces/55 grams of the Parmigiano-Reggiano and toss well to combine. Serve at once with additional cheese on the side.

MAKES 8 SIDE-DISH SERVINGS
OR 4 MAIN-DISH SERVINGS

Bathed in a tomato–basil sauce, richly layered with mozzarella, Italian sausage, and sweet peppers, stuffed and shaped into bite-size ravioli pillows or tortellini, or floating sublimely in a savoury vegetable soup, pasta is the equivalent of gastronomic pleasure. Whether the Italians invented it (or the Asians or Egyptians) we'll probably never know for sure. But pasta has been around for so long (over 7,000 years, according to pasta experts) that no one really cares exactly whence it came.

Pasta is at once both gourmet and soul food, economical and upscale, a child's delight and yet grand enough for royal fare. Perhaps no other food can deliver pleasure in so many interesting ways. It's amazing to think that a simple mixture of flour, water, and egg can be so versatile, such great food for the hungry soul. Pasta alone complements so many other savoury (and yes, sometimes sweet) foods that it would be difficult to name any other food that could serve in its place.

Cooking Tips

No matter which pasta you choose to serve, you need to start with a generous pan of water—at least 6½ pints/4 litres of rapidly boiling water. Add 1 teaspoon salt to the water, if desired. You may have heard that you should add olive or vegetable oil to the water to keep pasta from sticking together. It's not necessary to do this; simply using enough water and stirring the pot occasionally is enough to keep the pasta separated.

Add pasta gradually to the boiling water so the water continues to boil. Do not break long pastas when adding them to the pan. Instead, grip a handful of the pasta, such as spaghetti, at one end and dip the other end into the boiling water. The pasta will soften almost immediately, so that you can curve it around the bottom of the pan and stir in the entire length of the noodles.

Pasta should be cooked until it is tender but still slightly firm when you bite into it, a quality described by Italians as *al dente*. Begin testing the pasta to see if it is done a couple of minutes before the end of the suggested cooking time.

Pasta should be well drained the moment it is done. Never rinse pasta, except when it will be used in a cold pasta salad (this stops the cooking and chills the pasta quickly). Never place pasta in a bowl of water to cool; it will soften further and swell.

If you are not tossing the pasta immediately with sauce, 1 tablespoon of extra-virgin olive oil or butter per 1 pound/450 grams of cooked pasta can be tossed with the pasta after it is drained; this adds a note of flavour and keeps the pasta from sticking together before it is served. You can quickly re-heat pasta by dipping it, colander and all, into a pot of boiling water for 30 seconds; drain well and serve.

How Much Pasta to Cook?

DRY PACKAGED PASTA

Thin noodles. 1 pound/450 grams of dry packaged noodles makes 6 to 8 side-dish or starter servings, or 4 to 5 main-dish servings. One serving, 4 ounces/115 grams of dry spaghetti or fine noodles held together in a bunch, measures about 1 inch/2.5 centimetres in diameter.

4 ounces/115 grams dry spaghetti or fine noodles = 1 pound/450 grams cooked spaghetti

Macaroni or small pastas.

3½ ounces/100 grams of dry packaged macaroni or tiny pasta = 1½ pounds/675 grams cooked

Medium-wide noodles.

2 ounces of dry packaged medium noodles = 12 ounces/340 grams cooked

FRESH OR HOME-MADE PASTA

1 pound/450 grams of fresh pasta makes fewer servings than 1 pound/450 grams of dried pasta. If a serving size for dried pasta is 2 ounces/55 grams, the same serving calls for 3 ounces/85 grams of fresh pasta.

1 starter serving = 3 ounces/85 grams fresh pasta = 8 ounces/225 grams cooked pasta

1 main dish serving = 5 ounces/140 grams fresh pasta = 13 ounces/370 grams cooked pasta

1 pound/450 grams fresh pasta = about 5 to 6 starter servings or 3 main-dish servings

1⅓ pounds/620 grams fresh pasta = 1 pound/450 grams dried pasta

Pasta Shapes

A pasta name speaks volumes, but what does it say? You don't have to be an Italian to find out. Use this handy guide to expand your pasta horizons!

SMALL SHAPES

Acini di pepe – small dots or peppercorns

Alphabet – tiny letter shapes

Anellini – tiny ring macaroni

Conchigliette – tiny shell macaroni

Couscous – tiny round grains that cook up like rice

Cravattini – little bow ties

Ditalini – tiny tubes or little thimbles

Farfalletti – little butterflies

Occhi di trota – trout's eyes (half the length of ditallini)

Orzo (also called rosamarina) – a Greek pasta shaped like rice

Spezziello – tiny tubes

Stellini – tiny star macaroni

Tripolini – tiny bow ties

LARGER SHAPES

Cavatelli – clam shells

Conchiglie – medium shell macaroni

Conchiglioni – large shell macaroni

Farfalle – bow ties

Gemelli – rope macaroni

Mostaccioli – bias-cut tubes, 2 in/5 cm long and 1/2 in/1.25 cm wide

Penne – bias-cut tubes, 2 in 5 cm long and 1/4 in/6 mm wide

Radiatori – little radiators

Rigatoni – ridged hollow tubes, 2 in/5 cm long

Rotelle – corkscrew

Ruote – wagon wheels

NOODLES

Angel hair – fine noodles

Fettuccine – medium-wide noodles

Fusilli – long corkscrew noodles

Lasagne – flat noodles with straight or curly edges, 2 to 3 in/5 to 8cm wide

Linguine – small tongues; thicker than spaghetti

Mafalde – 1/2-in/1.25 cm wide noodles with a ruffled edge

Pappardelle – 3/4-in/2 cm-wide noodles

Spaghetti – standard long noodles

Verdi – green noodles

Vermicelli – straight fine noodles

Wide noodles – 1/2 in/1.25 cm wide, usually egg pasta

Ziti – long thin tubular pasta

PASTAS USED FOR STUFFING

Agnolotti – half rounds

Cannelloni – large ridged tubes with bias-cut ends

Cappelletti – little hats

Cappelli di prete – priests' hats

Lumache – jumbo shells

Manicotti – large tubes

Orecchioni – large ears

Ravioli – little pillows

Tortellini – Italian hat shapes

t the back was a screened-in porch, and we went in that way and deposited my gear on the wooden floor. Lucy opened the door leading into the kitchen, and we were enveloped by the aroma of tomatoes and garlic. She looked baffled as she stared at Marino and the dive equipment.

"What the hell's going on?" she said.

I could tell she was upset. This had been our night to be alone, and we did not have special nights like this often in our complicated lives.

"It's a long story." I met her eyes.

We followed her inside, where a large pot was simmering on the stove. Nearby on the counter was a cutting board, and Lucy apparently had been slicing peppers and onions when we arrived. She was dressed in FBI sweats and ski socks and looked flawlessly healthy, but I could tell she had not been getting much sleep.

"There's a hose in the pantry, and just off the porch near a spigot is an empty plastic trash can," I said to Marino. "If you'd fill that, we can soak my gear."

"I'll help," Lucy said.

"You most certainly won't." I gave her a hug. "Not until we've visited for a minute."

We waited until Marino was outside, then I pulled her over to the stove and lifted the lid from the pot. A delicious steam rose and I felt happy.

"I can't believe you," I said. "God bless you."

"When you weren't back by four I figured I'd better make the sauce or we weren't going to be eating lasagne tonight."

"It might need a little more red wine. And maybe more basil and a pinch of salt. I was going to use artichokes instead of meat, although Marino won't be happy about that, but he can just eat prosciutto. How does that sound?" I returned the lid to the pot.

Lasagne with Marinara Sauce and Porcini Mushrooms

Kay, Lucy, and Marino find themselves together on a snowy New Year's Eve in a tiny coastal cottage belonging to Dr. Philip Mant, Kay's Deputy Chief Medical Examiner for Virginia's Tidewater district.

Kay's own Italian tradition of cooking a pasta dish, with all of the components prepared from scratch, is carried on this night by Lucy, who has marinara sauce bubbling on the stove when Kay and Marino arrive. While Kay prepares the meal, which will include Braided Country Bread (page 152) and Fig, Melon, and Prosciutto Salad (page 160), she sips a glass of Côte Rôtie. (This was my father's favourite wine. When I went to France in June 1992 to accept the French book award, the Prix du Roman d'Aventures, for Postmortem, I brought several cases back with me.) Lucy enjoys a bottle of Peroni, an Italian beer. With the meal, Kay serves a Chianti.

MAKE-AHEAD TIP: Prepare the lasagne up to the baking step. Cover the pan tightly with two layers of aluminium foil. Freeze. Bake it frozen (do not thaw) and covered for 2 hours in pre-heated 375°F/190°C/gas mark 5 oven. Uncover and bake 15 to 20 minutes longer, until bubbly.

SHORTCUT TIP: Instead of making your own pasta, purchase fresh pasta sheets from an Italian deli or gourmet shop, as Kay does when she's short on time. The sheets of pre-rolled pasta can be refrigerated for several days or kept in the freezer for future use.

1 pound/450 grams whole-milk mozzarella cheese (preferably fresh) or
   pre-grated mozzarella cheese

1/2 recipe Kay's Fresh Pasta (page 52), 9 ounces/255 grams (12 sheets)
   store-bought fresh pasta sheets, or 9 to 12 dried lasagne noodles
   (about 9 ounces/255 grams)

1 ounce/25 grams dried porcini mushrooms or 4 ounces/115 grams
   chopped trimmed fresh mushrooms

16 fluid ounces/455 millilitres water

1 pound/450 grams lean minced beef

2 green, red or yellow peppers, de-seeded and thinly sliced

9 ounces/255 grams sliced onions

4 cloves garlic, finely chopped

2 tablespoons olive oil

14 ounces/400 grams tinned artichoke hearts, drained and cut into
   1/2 inch/1.25 centimetre pieces (do not use marinated artichoke hearts)

2 tablespoons chopped fresh oregano

1 teaspoon crushed fennel seeds

1 teaspoon salt

1/2 teaspoon freshly ground pepper

28 fluid ounces/800 millilitres Kay's Marinara Sauce (page 150) or prepared
   marinara sauce

2 1/2 fluid ounces/70 millilitres dry red wine

2 pounds/900 grams or four 250g tubs ricotta cheese

2 very large eggs

4 ounces/115 grams freshly grated Parmigiano-Reggiano, plus additional for serving

1/4 ounce/7 grams chopped fresh basil

1/4 ounce/7 grams chopped fresh flat-leaf parsley

1. At least 4 hours ahead or up to overnight, drain the liquid from the fresh
   mozzarella, if using. Place the cheese in a strainer lined with a clean tea
   towel or a triple layer of kitchen paper, set over a large bowl, and place in

the refrigerator to drain. Pat the cheese dry and tear into small bits. Cover and refrigerate until needed.

2. If making Kay's Fresh Pasta, follow the instructions for rolling out the pasta, using 2 balls (one-half) of the dough for the lasagne noodles. Dry the pasta for 30 minutes as directed. Place the rolled-out pasta on a chopping board and cut into 2-inch-/5-centimetre-wide noodles. Separate the noodles and allow to dry for 2 hours. (If drying the pasta longer, cover with cling film or tea towels and set aside for up to 24 hours.)

3. In a small saucepan, combine the porcini mushrooms and water. Bring to the boil over medium-high heat; remove from the heat. Cover and let stand 15 minutes. Drain the mushrooms well and rinse under cool water to remove any excess grit. Drain well again and chop. Set aside.

4. In a large deep frying pan, brown the minced beef thoroughly over medium heat. Drain the meat well. Transfer to a double layer of kitchen paper and press out the excess fat. In the same frying pan, cook the peppers, onions, and garlic in the olive oil for about 5 minutes, until tender.

5. Stir in the minced beef, artichoke hearts, porcini or fresh mushrooms, oregano, fennel, salt, and pepper. Stir in marinara sauce and red wine; bring the mixture to the boil over medium-high heat. Reduce the heat to low and simmer, stirring occasionally, for 20 minutes.

6. To cook the pasta: *For home-made noodles.* In a large pan, bring 6½ pints/4 litres of salted water to the boil. Add the noodles and cook for 3 to 5 minutes, or until *al dente* (tender but still firm to the bite). Drain the pasta and transfer to a pan of cold water to stop the cooking. Drain well and pat the noodles dry with kitchen paper.

   For store-bought fresh pasta sheets that require pre-cooking. Add the pasta sheets, one at a time, to the boiling water and cook for 2 $\frac{1}{2}$ to 3 minutes, until *al dente* (tender but still firm to the bite). As each sheet is done, carefully remove with tongs and transfer to a large pan of cold water to stop the cooking. Drain well and pat the noodles dry with kitchen paper. Cut the pasta into 2-inch-/5-centimetre-wide strips.

For packaged dry pasta that requires pre-cooking. Cook according to the package directions; drain and place in a pan of cold water to stop the cooking. Pat dry with kitchen paper.

7. In a large bowl, stir together the ricotta cheese, eggs, 2 ounces/55 grams of the Parmigiano-Reggiano, and the basil until combined. Put the mozzarella cheese into a separate bowl.

8. Pre-heat the oven to 375°F/190°C/gas mark 5. Lightly oil a 13x9x2-inch/33x23x5-centimetre rectangular baking dish. Spoon a little marinara sauce mixture over bottom of dish. Arrange one-third of the noodles on top. Spoon one-third of the ricotta cheese mixture over the noodles, spreading evenly to cover the pasta. Spoon one-third of the remaining marinara sauce mixture over the ricotta layer. Sprinkle with one-third of the mozzarella. Repeat the layers two times. Sprinkle with the remaining Parmigiano-Reggiano and the parsley.

9. Place the baking dish on a sturdy rimmed baking tray to catch any drips. Cover the dish with aluminium foil. Bake for 45 minutes. Uncover and bake for 10 to 15 minutes longer, or until the top is just beginning to brown and the filling is bubbly. Let the lasagne rest for 5 minutes before serving. Cut into 6 or 8 squares, depending on appetites.

SERVES 6 TO 8

Variation

FETTUSAGNE: I discovered this wonderful variation quite by accident when I had only packaged fettuccine noodles on hand. Substitute 2 packages (9 ounces/255 grams each) store-bought fresh fettuccine noodles for the lasagne. Cook the noodles according to package directions, drain well, and layer the noodles as directed for the lasagne.

Kay's Marinara Sauce

Make this incredible sauce during the summer when tomatoes are at their peak. You will find nothing compares to the fresh, rich flavour of this sauce. It takes some time to make, but remember that all good things come to those who wait. If you are a teetotaler, use chicken or vegetable stock in place of the red wine.

There is one important thing to remember when cooking this sauce: use a non-aluminium saucepan. The acid in tomatoes reacts with aluminium and produces a discoloration and a metallic off-flavour.

Since Kay lives in Richmond, it's easy for her to visit farm stands in the summer to get the delicious regional variety of tomatoes called Hanover, but you can use any good beefsteak or Roma (plum) tomatoes.

You can use this sauce in recipes like the lasagnes or pizzas in this book, over your own favourite pasta, over a cheese omelette, on steamed fresh vegetables, or in any recipe that calls for a good dose of marinara sauce.

MAKE-AHEAD TIP: This sauce freezes very well—Kay's freezer is stocked with it so she can enjoy it year-round. Just use some good freezer containers with tight-fitting lids. Put 8 to 16 fluid ounces/225 to 455 millilitres of sauce in each container, and mark the top. Leave at least $^1/_2$ inch/1.25 centimetres of headspace at the top for expansion.

6 to 7 pounds/2.7 to 3 kilograms fresh ripe beefsteak or Roma (plum) tomatoes

2 tablespoons olive oil

12 ounces/340 grams chopped onions

4 cloves garlic, finely chopped

6 ounces/170 grams tomato purée

½ ounce/15 grams chopped fresh basil

2 to 3 tablespoons chopped fresh oregano

1 tablespoon salt

¼ teaspoon freshly ground pepper

2 bay leaves

4 fluid ounces/115 millilitres dry red wine

1. Peel, de-seed and chop the tomatoes; set aside. (For how-to, see Note on page 135.)

2. In a large saucepan, heat the olive oil over medium heat. Add the onions and garlic and cook for about 3 minutes, or until tender but not brown. (Note: Although the sauce cooks down to 3 pints/1.5 litres, using a large pan allows room for simmering and prevents spattering.) Stir in the tomatoes and all of the remaining ingredients except the red wine; bring to the boil over medium-high heat. Reduce the heat and simmer, covered, stirring frequently, for 20 minutes.

3. Stir in the red wine. Cook for 30 to 35 minutes longer, or until the sauce cooks down to a thick consistency. Remove the bay leaves.

4. Use the sauce as needed, or cool to room temperature, then freeze as directed in the headnote.

MAKES ABOUT 3 PINTS/1.5 LITRES

Braided Country Bread

Part of Kay's lasagne feast includes her home-made bread, a sumptuous braided loaf, enriched with high-gluten flour and flavoured with olive oil and honey. You can place the dough in the oven to rise as the recipe directs, or if the oven is already being used, cover the dough and place the bowl on a rack set over a bowl of hot water. Often the top of your cooker is slightly warm if the oven is going, so it's perfect for rising dough.

You'll find it's easier to make a neat braided loaf if you start braiding in the middle of the three ropes. Braid them together towards one end, seal the ends together, then turn the baking sheet around and braid the other half.

SHORTCUT TIP: If you don't want to fuss with braiding, divide the dough in half and shape each half into two 18-inch/46-centimetre ropes. Twist the two ropes, pressing the ends together to seal. Bake as directed.

28 to 30 ounces/800 to 850 grams high-gluten flour (see Note on
　　page 31) or strong plain white flour

2 sachets fast action dry yeast

2 teaspoons salt

12 fluid ounces/340 millilitres milk

4 fluid ounces/115 millilitres water

5 tablespoons olive oil

2 tablespoons honey

1 medium egg, lightly beaten

1. In a large bowl, stir together 10 ounces/280 grams of the flour, the yeast, and the salt. In a medium saucepan, combine the milk, water, 3 tablespoons oil, and honey. Heat the mixture over medium heat, stirring, until it is very warm (120° to 130°F/48°C to 54°C). Stir the liquid into the flour mixture, then stir in 8 ounces/225 grams of the remaining flour.

2. Stir the flour mixture until it is well combined and the mixture begins to leave the side of the bowl. Turn the dough out onto a generously floured work surface and gather into a ball. Knead for about 10 minutes, until it is soft, smooth, and elastic, adding enough of the remaining flour to keep the dough from sticking.

3. Place the dough in a large greased bowl and turn the dough to coat evenly. Cover the dough with cling film or a damp clean tea towel. Place the bowl on the lowest oven rack. Turn the oven on to the lowest setting for 1 minute; immediately turn the oven off. Let the dough rise for 30 to 40 minutes or until doubled in size.

4. Punch down the dough; on a lightly floured surface, knead the dough 10 times to release the air bubbles. Cover the dough; let rest for 10 minutes.

5. To shape the dough: on a lightly floured surface, divide the dough in half. Set aside half the dough. Divide the remaining half of the dough into thirds; shape each third into a 14-inch/35-centimetre rope. Place the three ropes, side by side, on a large greased baking sheet. Braid or plait the ropes together, pinching the ends together to seal. Repeat with the remaining half of the dough. Brush the loaf with the beaten egg, then with olive oil. Cover the loaves and let rise 20 to 25 minutes, or until doubled in size.

6. Meanwhile, pre-heat the oven to 375°F/190°C/gas mark 5. Bake the loaves for 20 to 25 minutes, or until golden brown and loaves sound hollow when lightly tapped on the bottom. Transfer the loaves to a wire rack to cool slightly. Serve the bread warm or at room temperature with butter or olive oil for dipping.

| MAKES TWO LOAVES |

Lasagne coi Carciofi

(Lasagne with Artichokes and Béchamel Sauce)

Kay promises to make Lucy this unforgettable green noodle and white sauce lasagne, with its mild, delicate flavour. The béchamel sauce and artichokes make this a sophisticated twist on the traditional—and perfect for a holiday meal or dinner party. Even though béchamel sauce sounds intimidating, it is merely a simple white sauce. This is one recipe, like Kay's other lasagne (page 146), where it's definitely worthwhile to use fresh mozzarella.

As Kay does, you will want to reserve this extraordinary lasagne for special times when you have the afternoon to spend in the kitchen cooking for those you love. One bite of this heavenly lasagne will tell you that it was well worth the effort.

MAKE-AHEAD TIP: *See Make-Ahead Tip for Lasagne with Marinara Sauce and Porcini Mushrooms (page 146).*

1 pound/450 grams whole-milk mozzarella cheese (preferably fresh) or pre-grated mozzarella cheese

½ recipe Kay's Fresh Spinach Pasta (page 55), or 9 ounces/255 grams store-bought fresh spinach pasta sheets, or 9 to 12 dried lasagne noodles (about 9 ounces/255 grams)

1 pound/450 grams sweet Italian sausage, casings removed

2 tablespoons olive oil

4 ounces/115 grams stemmed and sliced fresh shiitake mushrooms or trimmed and sliced mushrooms

6 ounces/170 grams chopped onions

3 cloves garlic, finely chopped

1 jar (12 ounces/340 grams) roasted red peppers, well drained and
thinly sliced

14 ounces/400 grams tinned or bottled artichoke bottoms or hearts,
drained and cut into $1/2$-inch/1.25-centimetre pieces

$1/4$ ounce/7 grams chopped fresh basil

Salt and freshly ground pepper

1 recipe Béchamel Sauce (page 157)

4 ounces/115 grams freshly grated Parmigiano-Reggiano

$1/4$ ounce/7 grams chopped fresh flat-leaf parsley

1. At least 4 hours ahead or up to overnight, drain the liquid from the fresh mozzarella, if using. Place the cheese in a strainer lined with a clean tea towel or a triple layer of kitchen paper, set over a large bowl, and place in the refrigerator to drain. Pat the cheese dry and tear into bits. Cover and refrigerate until needed.

2. If making Kay's Fresh Spinach Pasta, follow the instructions for rolling out the pasta, using 2 balls (one-half) of the dough for the lasagne noodles. Dry the pasta for 30 minutes as directed. Place the rolled-out pasta on a chopping board and cut into 2-inch-/5-centimetre-wide noodles. Separate the noodles and allow to dry for 2 hours. (If drying the pasta longer, cover with cling film or tea towels and dry up to 24 hours.)

3. To cook the pasta: *For home-made noodles.* In a large pan, bring 6½ pints/4 litres of salted water to the boil. Add the noodles and cook for 3 to 5 minutes, or until *al dente* (tender but still firm to the bite). Drain the pasta and transfer to a pan of cold water to stop the cooking. Drain well and pat the noodles dry with kitchen paper.

For store-bought fresh pasta sheets that require pre-cooking. Add the pasta sheets, one at a time, to the boiling water and cook for 2½ to 3 minutes, until *al dente* (tender but still firm to the bite). As each sheet is done, carefully remove it with tongs and transfer to a large pan of cold water to stop the cooking. Drain well and pat the noodles dry with kitchen paper. Cut into 2-inch-/5-centimetre-wide strips.

For packaged dry pasta that requires pre-cooking. Cook according to the package directions, drain, and place in a pan of cold water to stop the cooking. Pat dry with kitchen paper.

4. In a large frying pan, crumble the sausage and cook over medium-high heat, for about 8 minutes, until browned. Drain well. Transfer the sausage to a double layer of kitchen paper and press out the excess fat. Wipe out the frying pan.

5. In the same pan, heat the olive oil over medium-high heat. Add the mushrooms, onions, and garlic and cook for about 5 minutes, or until the vegetables are tender. Stir in the roasted peppers, artichokes, sausage, and basil; season with salt and pepper. Remove from the heat. Transfer the mixture to a colander and drain off all the excess liquid. Cover and set aside.

6. Prepare the béchamel sauce (page 157). Cover and remove from the heat. Pre-heat the oven to 375°F/190°C/gas mark 5. Lightly oil a 13x9x2-inch/33x23x5-centimetre rectangular baking dish.

7. Spread 4 fluid ounces/115 millilitres of the béchamel sauce over the bottom of the dish. Arrange one-third of the noodles over the sauce, spreading evenly to cover. Top with half of the sausage and vegetable mixture; sprinkle with 4 ounces/115 grams of the mozzarella and $1^1/_4$ ounces/35 grams of the Parmigiano-Reggiano. Arrange another layer of noodles over the cheese, then top with the remaining sausage mixture, 4 ounces/115 grams mozzarella, and $1^1/_4$ ounces/35 grams of the Parmigiano-Reggiano. Arrange remaining noodles on top. Spread with the remaining béchamel sauce. Sprinkle the remaining 8 ounces/225 grams mozzarella and $1^1/_2$ ounces/45 grams Parmigiano-Reggiano evenly over the top. Sprinkle with parsley.

8. Place the baking dish on a sturdy rimmed baking tray to catch any drips. Bake for 45 to 50 minutes, until the top is browned and the filling is bubbly.

9. To serve, let the lasagne rest, covered, for 5 minutes before cutting. Cut into 6 or 8 squares, depending on appetites.

SERVES 6 TO 8

Béchamel Sauce

Béchamel is classic French white sauce. This version is a bit unusual because both cream and chicken stock are added. Use this recipe to make the Lasagne coi Carciofi (page 154), or you can jazz up Kay's lasagne (page 146) by substituting this sauce for half of the marinara sauce in the recipe. It's also an elegant drape for steamed fresh asparagus or broccoli.

2½ ounces/70 grams butter

5 tablespoons plain flour

12 fluid ounces/340 millilitres single cream (or use half single cream
    and half milk if you prefer a less rich sauce)

8 fluid ounces/225 millilitres chicken stock

¼ teaspoon salt

¼ teaspoon ground nutmeg

⅛ teaspoon ground white pepper

1. In a medium saucepan, melt the butter over medium-low heat; stir in the flour. Cook, stirring constantly, for about 3 minutes, until the mixture thickens and becomes golden in colour.

2. Stir in the cream and chicken stock all at once, whisking the mixture until smooth. Cook over medium heat, stirring constantly, for about 5 minutes, until the mixture comes to the boil. Reduce the heat to low and simmer for 2 minutes longer. Stir in the salt, nutmeg, and pepper.

3. Remove from the heat. Press a piece of greaseproof paper directly onto the surface to prevent a skin from forming.

MAKES 1 PINT/570 MILLILITRES

Kay's freezer provides her with a wonderful back-up for long work days and times when she has unexpected guests, such as Marino or Lucy. For cooks like Kay, who prepare food in generous amounts when time allows, freezing the leftovers is a great way to save time. And freezing, done correctly and promptly after food is prepared, won't alter the texture or taste of the food.

Start with good-quality freezer containers with tight-fitting lids or self-sealing freezer bags to preserve your bounty. Leave at least $1/2$ to 1 inch/1.25 to 2.5 centimetres of headspace at the top of the containers to allow for expansion during freezing, or fill freezer bags only three-quarters full for the same reason. If you are freezing a casserole in a baking dish, wrap the dish in heavy-duty aluminium foil (use two layers) and seal the edges securely with freezer tape (available in gourmet food and kitchen shops). Always be sure to label the containers, freezer bags, and packages with the date and the contents; the number of servings is also helpful.

Be sure food is cool before placing it in your freezer (a casserole hot from the oven will disrupt the operation of your freezer and delay freezing long enough to endanger the quality of your food). Don't overfill your freezer by stacking it to the top; leave enough room for the air to circulate. The food will freeze faster and the freezer temperature will be maintained. Here's a little-known tip: freezers operate more efficiently when they are filled to at least half-capacity. Your freezer should be set at 0°F/−18°C.

Thawing Tips

Food safety experts recommend three ways to defrost frozen foods. Use the one that is most convenient for you.

- Place the frozen food in the refrigerator. Allow it to thaw at least overnight or up to several days for larger items. To defrost a turkey, here's an easy guide: allow one day for every 5 pounds/2.25 kilograms. (A 20-pound/9-kilogram turkey will take about four days to thaw.)

◆ Place the food in a leakproof bag, and place the bag in the sink or in a large bowl of very cold water. Replace the water at least every 30 minutes to maintain the temperature; then refrigerate the food as soon as it thaws.

◆ Thaw the frozen food using your microwave oven. Refer to the manual for specific instructions. Plan to cook microwave-thawed food immediately after micro-thawing, as some portions of the food may have begun cooking during the defrosting.

Foods for the Freezer

Below is a list of foods that freeze very well, many of which you would find if you were to look in Kay's freezer. (Foods that don't freeze well include tinned foods, foods that are tossed in mayonnaise or cream dressings, lettuce, custard-type puddings and desserts, and cream sauces.)

- Breads, rolls, bagels, pizza
- Cookies, cakes, cheesecakes, fruit pies
- Fresh pasta dough, rolled pasta sheets, cooked pasta in casseroles, such as lasagne, filled pastas (cooked or uncooked), such as ravioli and tortellini
- Sauces, including marinara, bolognese, vegetable-based sauces
- Stews, soups, chilli, and strained chicken, beef, fish, or vegetable stocks
- Fresh fruit, except for kiwi fruit, bananas
- Fish, poultry, or meat casseroles
- Chopped or sliced fresh vegetables, such as summer squash, beans, peas, aubergines, onions, peppers, broccoli, cauliflower, carrots

Fig, Melon and Prosciutto Salad

This salad is an Italian classic, often served as a separate course as part of a pasta meal. However, there's no reason why this salad couldn't be a meal in itself, if arranged on a large platter with some extra prosciutto and served with a crusty loaf of bread and a chilled chardonnay or white Burgundy wine. It's a special treat for dining alfresco and reason enough to go on a romantic picnic.

In Cause of Death, Kay prepares this appetizer to serve with the New Year's Eve dinner she's sharing with Lucy and Marino at Dr. Mant's house.

Try to find a good source for the prosciutto. Have it freshly sliced in your supermarket, or seek out a great gourmet shop or Italian deli, where you'll have a variety of prosciuttos to choose from. (At Kay's house, Marino always gets extra prosciutto on his salad.)

Fresh figs are in season during the summer months and then again from November through to January. They may be dark purple, reddish brown, bright green, or greenish yellow, depending on the variety. When fresh figs are not to be had, you can substitute dried brown or mission figs, quartered.

MAKE-AHEAD TIP: This salad can be made up to a day ahead; assemble it on a pretty serving platter, then cover and chill for up to 24 hours before serving.

6 to 8 fresh figs

½ of a large ripe cantaloupe melon, de-seeded

Lettuce leaves, to serve

12 slices prosciutto (about 4½ ounces/130 grams)

Dijon mustard, for serving

1. Remove the stems from the figs and cut them into quarters. Cut the melon into quarters and cut off the rind. Cut each quarter into two wedges, then cut crosswise in half.

2. To serve, line four salad plates with lettuce leaves. Arrange the figs and melon slices decoratively over the lettuce. Separate the prosciutto slices and fold each slice in half or roll up. Arrange three slices on each salad. Serve with the Dijon mustard.

| SERVES 4 |

Fresh Fruit Salad
with Blood Orange Dressing

I n one of her frequent attempts to prod Marino into improving his diet, Kay devises this beautiful fruit salad for his breakfast one morning. When Marino says with disgust, "This ain't food. And what the hell are these little green slices with black things?" Kay patiently replies, "The kiwi fruit I told you to get. I'm sure you must have had it before." Marino brightens up when Kay produces bagels from her freezer and cream cheese. As usual, he's had a long night, so he is relieved when Kay pours caffeine-laden Guatemalan coffee, just the way he likes it. You might choose café au lait or a flavoured tea instead.

Blood oranges are an exotic variety of orange with a raspberry red interior and a reddish orange blush on the skin. Their flavour is rich and intense, like raspberry and orange combined, and they make a very attractive addition to salads and fruit compotes. Look for them in better markets that sell exotic produce.

4 blood oranges or navel oranges

4 ounces/115 grams red or green seedless grapes, halved

3 kiwi fruit, peeled, halved crosswise, and sliced

5 ounces/140 grams sliced strawberries, blueberries, or raspberries

Blood Orange Dressing:

2 tablespoons blood orange juice or orange juice

1 tablespoon olive oil

1 teaspoon finely grated blood orange or navel orange zest

1 teaspoon honey

Fresh mint leaves, for garnish

1. Reserve one of the oranges for the dressing. Peel the remaining oranges and slice thinly. Arrange the orange slices on four salad plates. Top with the grapes, kiwi fruit, and berries.

2. For the dressing: in a jar with a tight-fitting lid, combine the orange juice, olive oil, orange zest, and honey; shake well. Drizzle the dressing over the salads and garnish with mint leaves.

SERVES 4

Classic English Breakfast

(Bacon and Eggs with Tomatoes and Mushrooms)

The far-reaching case of Temple Gault takes Kay and Benton Wesley to London. Jet lag, lack of sleep, and raging appetites lead them further to breakfast at Richoux, a small, pretty restaurant at 41a South Audley Street in Mayfair. For the past ninety-odd years, Richoux has been famous for its all-day breakfast and traditional afternoon tea. (I discovered Richoux's beautiful French pastries and chocolates when I had a flat in London several years ago.)

This recipe for Classic English Breakfast is a hearty plateful of British Cumberland sausages, bacon, eggs, mushrooms, tomatoes, and toasted bread. The delectable sausages hail from the former county of Cumberland (now Cumbria) in northern England. However, your favourite fresh pork sausage is a very acceptable substitute.

Though Richoux toasts the bread for this breakfast, traditional Brits fry their bread in the same pan after cooking their bacon and eggs. Consider this breakfast a Marino special gone English, and you'll get the idea.

1 tablespoon butter

2 ounces/55 grams small mushrooms, trimmed

4 slices thick-cut bacon

2 Cumberland or other pork sausages

2 Roma (plum) tomatoes, halved or 1 medium tomato, cut into 4
   thick slices

4 very large eggs

2 thick slices white or French bread, halved diagonally

1. In a large frying pan, melt the butter over medium-high heat. Add the mushrooms and cook for about 3 minutes, or until browned. Transfer the mushrooms to a plate; keep warm.

2. In the same pan, fry the bacon for about 5 minutes, until crisp and brown, turning once; transfer to a kitchen paper-lined plate to drain. Pour off the pan juices; add the sausages to the pan and cook over medium heat for about 10–15 minutes, or until thoroughly cooked through, turning occasionally. Transfer the sausages to a plate to drain.

3. Pour the fat from the frying pan into a separate dish; return 1 teaspoon of the fat to the pan and fry the tomatoes for 3 minutes per side. Arrange the tomatoes on two breakfast plates.

4. Add 1 tablespoon sausage fat to the frying pan; fry the eggs over medium-low heat until cooked as desired. Arrange the eggs on the plates.

5. In the same pan, quickly fry the bread slices for 1 to 2 minutes, turning once, until golden brown, adding more sausage fat if necessary. Arrange the hot bread slices, bacon, sausages, and mushrooms on the plates Serve immediately.

SERVES 2

Unnatural Exposure

A shadow passed over her face as she opened a jar of horseradish. "I'm afraid I can imagine what you've been doing," she said. "Been hearing it on the news." She shook her head. "You must be plumb worn out. I don't know how you sleep. Let me tell you what to do for yourself tonight."

She walked over to a case of chilled blue crabs. Without asking, she selected a pound of meat in a carton.

"Fresh from Tangier Island. Hand-picked it myself, and you tell me if you find even a trace of cartilage or shell. You're not eating alone, are you?" she said.

"No."

"That's good to hear."

She winked at me. I had brought Wesley in here before.

She picked out six jumbo shrimp, peeled and deveined, and wrapped them. Then she set a jar of her homemade cocktail sauce on the counter by the cash register.

"I got a little carried away with the horseradish," she said, "so it will make your eyes water, but it's good." She began ringing up my purchases. "You sauté the shrimp so quick their butts barely hit the pan, got it? Chill 'em, and have that as an appetizer. By the way, those and the sauce are on the house."

"You don't need to . . ."

She waved me off. "As for the crab, honey, listen up. One egg slightly beaten, one-half teaspoon dry mustard, a dash or two of Worcestershire sauce, four unsalted soda crackers, crushed. Chop up an onion, a Vidalia if you're still hoarding any from summer. One green pepper, chop that. A teaspoon or two of parsley, salt and pepper to taste."

"Sounds fabulous," I gratefully said. "Bev, what would I do without you?"

"Now you gently mix all that together and shape it into patties." She made the motion with her hands. "Sauté in oil over medium heat until lightly browned. Maybe fix him a salad or get some of my slaw," she said. "And that's as much as I would fuss over any man."

Kay's Stew with Red Wine and Garlic

O n a balmy Halloween day, Kay puts on a pot of her home-made stew, which simmers through the afternoon in anticipation of a dinner with Marino. This is actually an adaptation of one of my own signature dishes—a rich, generous stew of vegetables, veal or beef chunks, garlic, Italian seasonings, and a lot of Gallo red Burgundy wine. I say adaptation because my stew never turns out exactly the same way twice, since the choice of meat and vegetables is different every time. I love to make a pot of this richly satisfying stew for friends, often creating a gift basket with a loaf of home-made bread and a bottle of good French Burgundy. To me, nothing is more special than a gift made with your own hands—it's a direct expression of the heart. I've even flown this stew, packed in dry ice, in my helicopter to friends, including Ruth and Billy Graham and Senator Orrin Hatch. (It didn't make it past Senate security initially, and when it did, Senator Hatch called and said, "I only got one bite—my staff ate it all.")

The secret to the deep, earthy flavours that develop in this stew comes from the careful browning of the meat cubes and the vegetables. Dredging the meat in flour encourages a nice brown crust and also helps thicken the stew later on. So don't skimp on the browning steps; keep cooking and stirring until you have achieved a nice deep golden brown colour on the meat and the vegetables.

Allow yourself a leisurely afternoon to make this stew, and you will be rewarded with a highly soul-satisfying meal in a bowl. The ingredient list for this wonderful stew may seem daunting, but all of the elements of this stew are simple to prepare. In preparation for this dish, spend a quick half hour doing the *ingredient chopping at the beginning; then it's a simple matter of adding every-thing at the appropriate time. As Kay does on this Indian summer day, you may want to serve the stew with Braided Country Bread (page 152).*

2 pounds/900 grams boneless veal shoulder or braising/stewing steak, trimmed of fat and cut into 1-inch/2.5-centimetre cubes

4 tablespoons plain flour

4 tablespoons olive oil

1 large onion, cut into 1-inch/2.5-centimetre wedges

4 cloves garlic, finely chopped

6 ounces/170 grams chopped carrots (= 2 carrots)

4 ounces/115 grams sliced celery (= 2 sticks celery)

16 fluid ounces/455 millilitres red Burgundy wine

16 fluid ounces/455 millilitres home-made beef stock or ready-made beef stock

8 fluid ounces/225 millilitres V-8 juice

8 fluid ounces/225 millilitres tomato sauce or passata

2 tablespoons chopped fresh basil

1 tablespoon chopped fresh oregano

1 tablespoon chopped fresh thyme

2 bay leaves

1 ½ teaspoons salt

¼ teaspoon freshly ground pepper

8 ounces/225 grams mushrooms, trimmed and sliced

14 ounces/400 grams tinned or bottled artichoke hearts, drained and halved

8 ounces/225 grams asparagus, trimmed and cut into 1-inch/2.5-centimetre lengths

6 ounces/170 grams diced peeled potatoes

8 ounces/225 grams shelled fresh peas or frozen peas

3 tablespoons chopped fresh parsley, for garnish

1. Place the veal or beef cubes in a large self-sealing bag with the flour. Seal the bag and shake well to coat the meat with the flour. In a large, heavy-based saucepan or flameproof casserole dish, heat 2 tablespoons of the oil over medium-high heat. Brown the meat cubes on all sides, turning frequently, for about 10 minutes, or until meat is a deep golden brown. Make sure that the pan is always hot enough to sizzle the meat and the vegetables, but not so hot that they burn and stick to the pan. Remove meat from the pan.

2. Add 1 tablespoon oil to the pan. Add the onion and garlic and cook over medium-high heat, stirring frequently, for about 8 minutes, or until deep golden brown. Transfer the onion mixture to a dish. Add the remaining 1 tablespoon oil to the pan; add the carrots and celery and cook over medium-high heat, stirring frequently, for about 8 minutes, until deep golden brown.

3. Return the meat and onion mixture to the pan. Add 8 fluid ounces/225 millilitres of the red wine, the beef stock, and V-8 juice, scraping up the crusty browned bits of meat and vegetables from the bottom of the pan so they can meld with the liquid. Stir in the tomato sauce or passata, basil, oregano, thyme, bay leaves, salt, and pepper until well blended. Bring the mixture to the boil over high heat, then reduce heat to low and simmer gently, uncovered, stirring occasionally, for 1½ hours.

4. Stir in the remaining wine, the mushrooms, artichoke hearts, asparagus, potatoes, and peas. Simmer for 1 to 1½ hours longer, or until the meat is very tender.

5. Taste for seasoning and remove the bay leaves. Ladle the stew into shallow serving bowls and sprinkle with the parsley.

SERVES 6 TO 8

THE VERSATILE TOMATO: *BELLISSIMO!*

What would great Italian cooking be without the tomato? Chopped up for a fresh pasta sauce, simmered in a creamy soup, puréed and spread over a pizza crust, nestled with garlic and herbs for a killer bruschetta, or layered with fresh mozzarella cheese and sprinkled with balsamic vinegar—the culinary opportunities are endless! Hot or cold, fresh off the vine, puréed, crushed, stewed, stuffed, or dried, there is hardly a more versatile fruit than the tomato.

Tomato Varieties

Take your pick from the harvest of tomatoes available in food markets, farmers' markets, supermarkets, gourmet catalogues, or at your local nursery.

BEEFSTEAK — a large tomato with broad "shoulders" or knobs near the stem; perfect for sandwiches, salads, and flavourful sauces.

ROMA (PLUM) — a small, oval or pear-shaped tomato that is very meaty. Ideal for cutting into wedges or slices, chopping for vegetable mixtures, or for sauces.

CHERRY — miniature round tomatoes, available in both golden and red varieties. Great for salads, appetizers, vegetable platters.

GOLDEN — "yellow" tomato with a golden yellow skin and flesh, available as large tomatoes, cherry tomatoes, or as a grape or pear tomato. It has a sweet flavour and is as versatile as the red tomato.

GRAPE — smaller than cherry tomatoes, with an elongated round shape like a grape; available in red and golden varieties. Use as substitute for cherry tomatoes.

GREEN — an unripe red tomato. Coat and batter-fry or use in sauces.

ORANGE — a tomato hybrid with orange skin and flesh; sweet in flavour. Use as you would a red tomato.

PEAR — or "teardrop" tomato; a small cherry tomato with a pear shape. In yellow and red varieties. Use as substitute for cherry tomatoes.

ROUND RED — more medium sized and rounder than a beefsteak tomato, most common variety available. A good slicing and all-purpose tomato.

VINE-RIPENED — medium-sized red tomatoes with the vine and stems still attached. These tomatoes have tender skins and should be used within a couple of days for best flavour. As versatile as any tomato.

Buying and Storing Fresh Tomatoes

Buy tomatoes with smooth rich red (or gold or orange) skins that have a subtle sweet scent and yield slightly with gentle pressure when held between your palms. Avoid bruised or split tomatoes, or hard, pale pink-skinned winter tomatoes; if that's all you see in your supermarket's produce aisle, then do as Kay does in a pinch— look for hothouse tomatoes (sometimes called Holland tomatoes or tomatoes-on-the-vine), or opt for a tinned product, instead.

MEASUREMENT EQUIVALENTS:

2 large or 3 medium tomatoes = 1 pound/450 grams

8 to 9 Roma (plum) tomatoes or 24 cherry tomatoes = 1 pound/450 grams

1 medium tomato or 6 cherry tomatoes = 1 serving

There are two things to remember when storing tomatoes: never ripen tomatoes in sunlight (which only makes them mushy), and never refrigerate tomatoes unless they are very ripe and you don't plan to use them for several days (chilling them does nothing to develop the flavour). Tomatoes ripen naturally and develop their flavour when kept out of sunlight in temperatures between 50° and 60°F/10° and 15°C. Rotate your tomato supply and use the ripest ones first, as you do bananas. You can speed up the ripening by placing the tomatoes in a fruit-ripening bowl (available in speciality kitchen shops and catalogues) or in a paper produce bag, but be sure to check their progress daily.

Tomatoes for Your Store-Cupboard

During the winter season, it's perfectly fine to rely on tinned and packaged tomato purée and sauces, which are processed when tomatoes are at their peak. These are also very convenient products to use when time is too short to cook fresh tomatoes. Here's a condensed list of what you'll find on your supermarket shelf:

- crushed tomatoes in tomato purée
- diced or chopped tomatoes
- whole peeled tomatoes
- Italian-style tomatoes with herbs and garlic
- chunky-style or "pasta-ready" tomatoes
- low-sodium tomato products
- tomato purée
- tomato sauce or passata
- sun-dried tomatoes, packed dry or in oil

Jumbo Shrimps with Bev's Kicked by a Horse Cocktail Sauce

Kay heads for home in a heavy rain, anticipating dinner at her house with Wesley. She takes the turnoff to Carytown, a shopping district in Richmond, to buy some shrimps and fresh crabmeat at P. T. Hasting's Famous Seafood. This seafood shop, with two Richmond locations at 3545 West Cary Street and 8128 West Broad Street, offers an abundance of top-quality local fish and seafood.

Bev, the kind lady behind the counter, picks out six jumbo shrimps for Kay's tête-à-tête with Wesley. Kay also picks up a jar of Bev's Kicked by a Horse Cocktail Sauce to accompany the shrimps. Both Bev's character and the cocktail sauce were fictional when Unnatural Exposure was published, but after P. T. Hasting, Jr., the proprietor, and his staff received so many inquiries about the non-existent sauce, they started making and selling it.

Bev's cooking advice for the shrimps is summed up succinctly this way: "You sauté the shrimps so quick their butts barely hit the pan, got it? Chill 'em and have that as an appetizer." Enough said.

6 jumbo shrimps, peeled and de-veined
1 tablespoon olive oil

Cocktail Sauce:

4 fluid ounces/115 millilitres tomato ketchup

2 tablespoons prepared horseradish sauce

$\frac{1}{2}$ teaspoon Worcestershire sauce

Few dashes of hot pepper sauce

1 teaspoon fresh lemon juice

Lettuce leaves and/or crushed ice, for serving

Lemon or lime wedges, for garnish

1. Rinse the shrimps and pat dry. In a small frying pan, heat the oil over medium-high heat. Add the shrimps and cook, turning frequently, for about 3 minutes, or until they turn pink and opaque throughout. Immediately remove the pan from the heat and transfer the shrimps to a plate. Cover and chill at least 1 hour or up to 24 hours before serving.

2. For the cocktail sauce: in a small bowl, stir together the tomato ketchup, horseradish sauce, Worcestershire sauce, hot pepper sauce, and lemon juice. Cover and chill until serving time.

3. To serve, arrange the shrimps over lettuce leaves and/or crushed ice with lemon or lime wedges. Serve along with the cocktail sauce for dipping.

MAKES 2 STARTER SERVINGS

Bev's Lump Crab Cakes

These delicate crab cakes are an adaptation of the off-the-cuff recipe that counter clerk Bev gives Kay at P. T. Hasting's seafood shop in Carytown. If fresh lump crabmeat is expensive in your area, you can substitute tinned lump crabmeat—be sure to pick through for any small pieces of cartilage. (Lump refers to large pieces from the body.)

On Bev's recommendation, Kay likes to serve the crab cakes with coleslaw (you might try the Marinated Coleslaw with Apple Cider Vinaigrette on page 69) or a simple tossed salad. For an elegant touch, wrap lemon or lime halves in gauze wrappers (available in speciality food and kitchen shops) to decorate each plate. When the juice is squirted over the crab cakes, the wrappers act as a nifty catch-all for the citrus seeds and pulp.

Benton Wesley brings along a Cakebread chardonnay to drink that evening, but you could also try a white Burgundy.

3 large eggs, lightly beaten

2 tablespoons milk

1 teaspoon Worcestershire sauce

½ teaspoon dry mustard

1 pound/450 grams lump crabmeat or 4 tins (6 ounces/170 grams
    each) lump crabmeat, drained and picked over

5 ounces/140 grams fresh breadcrumbs

6 ounces/170 grams de-seeded and finely chopped green pepper (= 1 pepper)

3 ounces/85 grams finely chopped onion (= 1 small onion)

1 tablespoon chopped fresh parsley

½ teaspoon salt

¼ teaspoon freshly ground pepper

2 tablespoons olive oil

Lemon or lime wedges, for serving

1. In a large bowl, whisk together the eggs, milk, Worcestershire sauce, and dry mustard. Stir in the crabmeat, breadcrumbs, green pepper, onion, parsley, salt, and pepper and mix well to combine.
2. With your hands, carefully shape the crab mixture into eight round cakes, about 3½ inches/9 centimetres wide and 1 inch/2.5 centimetres thick.
3. In a large frying pan, heat the oil over medium-high heat. Add the crab cakes and cook for about 5 minutes per side, or until golden brown, turning the cakes carefully with a wide spatula to preserve their shape.
4. Serve the crab cakes hot with lemon or lime wedges.

MAKES 4 MAIN-DISH SERVINGS

(2 CRAB CAKES EACH)

OR 8 STARTER SERVINGS

(1 CRAB CAKE EACH)

Lila's Clam Stew

Kay finds a handwritten recipe for this stew on a discarded scrap of paper during her search of Lila Pruitt's house on Tangier Island, off the Virginia coast. Before her tragic death from smallpox, Lila made her living selling recipes on the sidewalk for a quarter (25 cents) each. This recipe for a wonderful clam and fish stew with an authentic island flavour might have been a bestseller for a character like Lila.

Though the ingredient list looks long and complicated, this is actually a very simple dump-in-the-pot stew that you can assemble in half an hour, and the cooking time totals only about 45 minutes. The blend of herbs, wine, and saffron flavours is reminiscent of bouillabaisse, but you'll find that the ingredients for this hearty concoction are much easier to come by. Serve the stew with slices of warm, crusty bread, a simple mixed-lettuce salad, and a spicy gewürztraminer, California chardonnay, or pinot gris wine.

3 tablespoons olive oil

8 ounces/225 grams mushrooms, trimmed and sliced

6 ounces/170 grams chopped celery

9 ounces/255 grams chopped carrots

6 ounces/170 grams chopped onions

3 cloves garlic, finely chopped

1 tin (28 ounces/800 grams) crushed tomatoes in purée or chopped
  tomatoes in juice

2 bottles (8 fluid ounces/225 mililitres each) clam juice

4 fluid ounces/115 millilitres dry white wine

2 tablespoons chopped fresh basil

1 tablespoon chopped fresh thyme

2 bay leaves

$1/2$ teaspoon salt

$1/4$ teaspoon crushed saffron threads

$1/8$ to $1/4$ teaspoon crushed red pepper flakes

1 pound/450 grams fish fillets (such as grouper, red snapper, halibut,
   white fish, or cod), cut into $1/2$-inch/1.25-centimetre chunks

$1^1/2$ to 2 dozen fresh littleneck clams in their shells, scrubbed

1. In a large saucepan, heat the oil over medium-high heat; add the mushrooms, celery, carrots, onions, and garlic and cook for 5 to 8 minutes, or until the vegetables are tender. Stir in the tomatoes with their purée or juice, clam juice, white wine, basil, thyme, bay leaves, salt, saffron, and crushed red pepper. Bring the mixture to the boil. Reduce the heat to low and simmer, uncovered, stirring occasionally, for 30 minutes.

2. Add the fish chunks to the stew; cook 5 minutes. Add the clams and cover the pan tightly. Simmer for 3 to 5 minutes, or until shells open, discarding any clams that do not open.

3. To serve, remove the bay leaves. Ladle the stew into large pasta or soup bowls.

SERVES 6 TO 7

ell, I think you look pretty cool, as Lucy would say. I've got coffee and granola."

"How many times do I got to tell you that I don't eat friggin' birdseed," he grumbled as he followed me through the house.

"And I don't cook steak-egg biscuits."

"Well, maybe if you did, you wouldn't spend so many evenings alone."

"I hadn't thought about that."

"Did the Smithsonian tell you where we was going to park up there? Because there's no parking in D.C."

"Nowhere in the entire district? The President should do something about that."

We were inside my kitchen, and the sun was gold on windows facing it, while the southern exposure caught the river glinting through trees. I had slept better last night, although I had no idea why, unless my brain had been so overloaded it simply had died. I remembered no dreams, and was grateful.

"I got a couple of VIP parking passes from the last time Clinton was in town," Marino said, helping himself to coffee. "Issued by the mayor's office."

He poured coffee for me, too, and slid the mug my way, like a mug of beer on the bar.

"I figured with your Benz and those, maybe the cops would think we have diplomatic immunity or something," he went on.

"I'm supposing you've seen the boots they put on cars up there."

I sliced a poppyseed bagel, then opened the refrigerator door to take an inventory.

"I've got Swiss, Vermont cheddar, prosciutto."

I opened another plastic drawer.

"And Parmigiano-Reggiano—that wouldn't be very good. No cream cheese. Sorry. But I think I've got honey, if you'd rather have that."

"What about a Vidalia onion?" he asked, looking over my shoulder.

"That I have."

"Swiss, proscuitto, and a slice of onion is just what the doctor ordered," Marino happily said. "Now that's what I call a breakfast."

"No butter," I told him. "I have to draw the line somewhere so I don't feel responsible for your sudden death."

"Deli mustard would be good," he said.

I spread spicy yellow mustard, then added prosciutto and onion with the cheese on top, and by the time the toaster oven had heated up, I was consumed by cravings. I fixed the same concoction for myself and poured my granola back into its tin. We sat at my kitchen table and drank Colombian coffee and ate while sunlight painted the flowers in my yard in vibrant hues, and the sky turned a brilliant blue.

Marino's Breakfast Bagel Sandwich

Before making a drive to Washington, D.C., with Marino, Kay offers him her standard-issue coffee and granola breakfast. When Marino announces to Kay that he simply won't eat "friggin' birdseed," Kay switches gears and produces a breakfast on a bagel that makes him much happier. "Now that's what I call a breakfast," says Marino with enthusiasm.

Kay admits, ". . . by the time the toaster oven had heated up, I was consumed by cravings. I fixed the same concoction for myself and poured my granola back into its tin." I often tell people I'm a mix of my characters—I'm mostly healthy like Kay, but sometimes I indulge in awfully fattening foods like Marino's favourites and the cookies that Lucy loves to bake so much. This bagel recipe, as Marino says, is just what the doctor ordered. Brew up some Colombian coffee to sip alongside.

1 poppyseed bagel, split and toasted

Butter or mayonnaise

6 slices prosciutto

2 slices (1/4 inch/6 millimetres thick) onion

2 slices Gruyère cheese

Spicy yellow mustard

1. Spread the toasted bagel halves with butter or mayonnaise. Arrange the bagel halves, cut side up, on a grill tray. Layer the prosciutto slices on top of one bagel half; top with onion and cheese slices.

2. Place the cheese-topped bagel half on a grill pan under a pre-heated grill, 4 inches/10 centimetres from the heat source, for about 1 to 1½ minutes, or just until cheese melts. Top with second bagel half. Serve the sandwich immediately with mustard.

SERVES 1

Grilled Chicken Caesar Salad

K ay treats Marino to dinner at the Old Ebbitt Grill, a Washington, D.C., institution that was founded in 1856. Known as the oldest saloon in the city, the restaurant actually began as a boarding house on the other side of town, purchased by innkeeper William E. Ebbitt. Many a distinguished name in history either lived there or tipped a few at the stand-up bar, including Presidents McKinley, Grant, Andrew Johnson, Cleveland, Teddy Roosevelt, and Warren G. Harding.

The Old Ebbitt Grill has occupied various locations in its lifetime, finally moving to its current address, a renovated theatre, at 675 15th Street NW. Its Victorian décor is punctuated by relics from the past, including beer steins, animal heads bagged by Teddy Roosevelt, and even some of Alexander Hamilton's wooden bears, which he is rumoured to have brought in for his own private bar.

Of course, Marino can't resist indulging in several pints of Samuel Adams brew along with his Gruyère cheese burger. Kay opts for the healthier Chicken Caesar Salad, a recipe that chef Tom Myer graciously shared with us. The Old Ebbitt serves large portions—this salad comes with a sliced double chicken breast on it. If Kay were to make this at home, she would use just one chicken breast per serving. If you don't wish to use raw egg in the dressing, you can substitute a hard-boiled egg, finely chopped.

Caesar Dressing:

1 large egg yolk or 1 hard-boiled egg, peeled and finely chopped

1 tablespoon Dijon mustard

2 anchovy fillets, drained and mashed

2 cloves garlic, finely chopped

5 fluid ounces/140 millilitres olive oil

4 tablespoons fresh lemon juice

1 tablespoon white wine vinegar

Salad:

4 skinless, boneless chicken breasts (about 1 1/2 pounds/675 grams
   total)

8 fluid ounces/225 millilitres bottled Italian-style salad dressing

1 large head romaine lettuce, trimmed and chopped

2 ounces/55 grams freshly grated Parmigiano-Reggiano

1. For the Caesar dressing: in a bowl, whisk together the egg yolk (or hard-boiled egg) and mustard. Mix in the anchovy fillets and garlic. While whisking, slowly pour in the olive oil in a thin stream, until blended. Whisk in the lemon juice and vinegar until the dressing is thick and well blended. Cover and refrigerate until needed.

2. In a shallow glass or ceramic dish, marinate the chicken breasts in Italian-style salad dressing for at least 1 hour or up to overnight. Drain the marinade from the chicken and discard.

3. To cook the chicken: pre-heat the barbecue to medium-hot or pre-heat the grill. Barbecue the chicken for 13 to 15 minutes, until the thickest part is no longer pink, turning once. (Or place chicken pieces on the oiled rack of a grill pan; grill 4 inches/10 centimetres from the heat source for 10 to 12 minutes, turning once.) Set the chicken aside to cool slightly.

4. Whisk the Caesar dressing and reserve 4 tablespoons. In a large bowl, toss together the lettuce, Parmigiano-Reggiano, and the remaining Caesar dressing. Divide the salad among four large dinner plates. Thinly slice each chicken breast and arrange the slices, overlapping, on the top of the salad. Drizzle the reserved dressing over the chicken. Serve immediately.

SERVES 4

Greek Salad with Red Wine Vinaigrette

O n their way to meet Lucy and her companion, Janet, at their apartment just off Dupont Circle in Washington, D.C., Kay and Marino stop to pick up some take-away. In the 2000 block of P Street, D.C. Café, a twenty-four-hour self-serve restaurant, seems to be just the ticket. On the menu are Greek and Mediterranean specialities, including gyros, pitta sandwiches, baklava, and Lebanese beer.

D.C. Café's owner, Ayman Almoualem, shares his version of Greek salad—a colourful mix of cucumbers, tomatoes, calamata olives, and feta cheese, laced with a minted red wine vinaigrette, a side dish that never fails to please customers. To make this an entrée salad, double the amount of feta cheese and/or add some slices of roasted lamb or beef.

MAKE-AHEAD TIP: Make the salad ahead, if you prefer, by refrigerating the salad mixture and the dressing separately for up to several hours. Toss the salad with the dressing just before serving.

Red Wine Vinaigrette:

6 fluid ounces/170 millilitres olive oil

4 fluid ounces/115 millilitres red wine vinegar

4 fluid ounces/115 millilitres fresh lemon juice

1 teaspoon crushed dried mint

1/2 teaspoon salt

1/4 teaspoon cracked black pepper

Salad:

5 ounces/140 grams torn romaine lettuce

3 ounces/85 grams mixed torn lettuce mix

4 ounces/115 grams shredded red cabbage

7 ounces/200 grams sliced cucumber (1 medium)

2 medium tomatoes, cut into thin wedges

6 ounces/170 grams sliced red onions

3 ounces/85 grams trimmed and sliced mushrooms

1 red pepper, thinly sliced

4 ounces/115 grams crumbled feta cheese

2 ounces/55 grams pitted and sliced calamata olives

1. For the Red Wine Vinaigrette: in a large jar with a tight-fitting lid, combine the oil, vinegar, lemon juice, mint, salt, and pepper. Cover and shake well; set aside.

2. For the salad: in a large salad bowl, toss together the romaine lettuce, lettuce mix, and cabbage. Add all the remaining ingredients and toss gently.

3. To serve the salad, shake the dressing, drizzle over the salad, and toss well. Serve immediately.

MAKES 6 TO 8 SIDE-DISH SERVINGS

Black Notice

We turned off the Boulevard des Italiens onto the Rue Favard. "I shouldn't be bitter when I was *sent* here to solve problems—when I've been a pawn in some scheme I knew nothing about?"

"I'm sorry you look at it that way," he said.

"We're bad for each other," I said.

Café Runtz was small and quiet, with green checked cloths and green glassware. Red lamps glowed and the chandelier was red. Odette was making a drink at the bar when we walked in. Her way of greeting Talley was to throw her hands up in despair and chastise him.

"She's accusing me of staying away two months and then not calling before I come in," he translated for me.

He leaned over the bar and kissed her on both cheeks to make amends. Regardless of how crowded the café was, she managed to fit us into a choice corner table because Talley had that effect on people. He was used to getting what he wanted. He picked out a Santenay red burgundy since he remembered I'd told him how much I like burgundies, although I didn't recall when I'd said that or if I really had. By now I wasn't sure what he already knew and what he'd gotten directly from me.

"Let's see," he said, scanning the menu. "I highly recommend the Alsacienne specialities. But to start? The *salade de gruyère*—shaved gruyère that looks like pasta on lettuce and tomato. It's filling, though."

Kay's Grilled Pizza with Sausage, Pepperoni and Three Cheeses

For this grilled version of pizza, it's imperative that you control the temperature of the grill. If the gas is turned up too high or the coals are too hot, the crust will burn on the bottom before the toppings warm up and the cheese melts. It's a simple matter to turn down the gas, but for a charcoal grill, use indirect heat. Before you arrange the coals, use a disposable foil drip pan placed in the centre of the firebox, just under where you will place the pizza on the grate. Then, using long tongs, arrange the coals in mounds around the drip pan. For this type of indirect-heat cooking, you'll need hot coals for a medium-hot effect. You can tell you have hot coals if, by holding your hand palm side down just above the grate, you need to remove your hand in the time it takes you to say, "one-thousand one, one-thousand-two."

If you prefer a crispy crust, turn the crust once after the first grilling before adding the topping ingredients. Also see Kay's recipe for baked pizza on page 28.

12 ounces/340 grams whole-milk mozzarella cheese (preferably fresh) or pre-grated mozzarella cheese

Pizza Dough:

1 teaspoon fast action dry yeast

4 fluid ounces/115 millilitres warm water (110° to 115°F/43 to 46°C)

1 tablespoon honey

12 to 13 ounces/340 to 370 grams high-gluten flour (see Note on
    page 31) or strong plain white flour

1 tablespoon olive oil

1 teaspoon salt

Topping:

3 tablespoons olive oil

1 green, red or yellow pepper, de-seeded and thinly sliced

1 portobello mushroom, stem removed, quartered and thinly sliced or
    5 ounces/140 grams trimmed and sliced mushrooms

6 ounces/170 grams sliced onions

3 cloves garlic, finely chopped

Salt and freshly ground pepper

8 ounces /225 grams sweet Italian sausage

12 fluid ounces/340 millilitres Kay's Marinara Sauce (page 150),
    prepared marinara sauce or Quick Marinara Sauce (page 31)

8 ounces/225 grams sliced turkey pepperoni

$1/4$ ounce/7 grams chopped fresh basil

4 ounces/115 grams grated fontina cheese

2 ounces/55 grams freshly grated Parmigiano-Reggiano

1. At least 4 hours ahead or up to overnight, drain the liquid from the fresh mozzarella, if using. Place the cheese in a strainer lined with a clean tea towel or a triple layer of kitchen paper, set over a large bowl, and place in the refrigerator to drain. Pat the cheese dry and tear into bits. Cover and refrigerate until needed.

2. For the pizza dough: in a large bowl, dissolve the yeast in the warm water; stir in the honey. Stir in 10 ounces/280 grams of the flour, the oil, and salt until moistened. Stir in enough additional flour so the mixture leaves the side of the bowl. Turn the dough out onto a lightly floured surface and gather it into a ball. Knead the dough for about 10 minutes, until the dough is soft, smooth, and elastic, adding enough of the remaining flour to keep the dough from sticking.

3. Place the dough in a large greased bowl and turn the dough to coat evenly. Cover the dough with cling film or a damp clean tea towel. Place the bowl on the lowest oven rack. Turn the oven on to the lowest setting for 1 minute; immediately turn the oven off. Let the dough rise for about 30 minutes, or until doubled in size.

4. Punch down the dough; on a lightly floured surface, knead the dough 10 times to release the air bubbles. Cover the dough and let it rest while making the topping.

5. For the topping: in a large frying pan, heat 2 tablespoons of the olive oil over medium-high heat; add the pepper, mushroom, onions, and garlic and cook for about 5 minutes, or until very tender. Transfer the vegetables to a colander to drain well. Season with salt and pepper. Wipe the pan dry. In the same frying pan, crumble the sausage and cook over medium-high heat for about 8 minutes, or until browned. Transfer to kitchen paper to drain.

6. To grill the pizzas: pre-heat the grill. Cut the pizza dough in half; shape each half into a ball. Flatten each dough ball with the palm of your hand; roll or pat into a 12-inch/30 centimetre round. Lightly brush the top of the dough with olive oil. Place each crust on a separate large rimless baking sheet. Using the baking sheet like a large spatula, slide one of the crusts under the grill; cook for 2 to 3 minutes, or until the bottom of the crust is lightly browned and the top of the crust begins to puff. Remove from the grill; repeat with the second crust.

7. If the crusts are still puffed on the top, flatten them with a metal spatula. Spread the marinara sauce evenly over the crusts. Top with the sausage, pepperoni, and vegetable mixture, dividing them evenly. Sprinkle with the basil, then top with the mozzarella, fontina, and Parmigiano-Reggiano.

8. Return the pizzas to the grill and cover them loosely with aluminium foil. Grill for 4 to 6 minutes longer, or until the toppings are hot and the cheeses melt. Using a large spatula, transfer the pizzas to the baking sheets. Serve immediately, cut into wedges.

MAKES TWO 12-INCH/30-CENTIMETRE PIZZAS

Rose's Vegetable Soup with Italian Herbs

K ay's loyal secretary, Rose, about whom we know very little until this revealing scene in Black Notice, *turns out to have a dynamite recipe for vegetable soup. She shares a frozen container of the soup with her tired boss, knowing that this Christmas is an exceptionally difficult one for Kay.*

This soup has an old-fashioned flavour that is intended to warm the cockles of your heart, as it did Kay's. It's very important to remove all the sand and grit before slicing the leeks. Trim off a slice from the root, then trim off the green leaves to within 2 inches/5 centimetres of the white part of the leeks. Split the leaves apart down to the white portion of the leek, and wash the leaves and the white part under cold running water until you have rinsed away all of the dirt. Cut off the green leaves down to the white and discard them. Then thinly slice the white portion.

Choose a combination of your favourite vegetables to make the soup. It cooks in just under an hour.

MAKE-AHEAD TIP: *Like Rose, you can freeze the soup after it cools, in meal-sized portions; just use freezer-safe containers.*

SHORTCUT TIP: *You can substitute frozen loose-pack vegetables for most of the fresh vegetables listed, except the cabbage, celery, and mushrooms.*

3 tablespoons olive oil

6 ounces/170 grams de-seeded and chopped green, red or yellow pepper

2 leeks, sliced (white part only)

3 cloves garlic, finely chopped

3 pints/1.5 litres home-made vegetable stock or ready-made vegetable
  stock

1 tin (14 ounces/400 grams) Italian-style chopped tomatoes in juice

4 to 4½ pounds/1.75 to 2 kilograms fresh vegetables in any combination
  (broccoli or cauliflower florets; shredded cabbage; yellow or green beans
  or asparagus cut into 1-inch/2.5-centimetre lengths; thinly sliced carrots,
  fennel, or parsnips; baby sweet corn; sliced celery; trimmed and sliced
  button mushrooms; or fresh or frozen peas)

¼ ounce/7 grams chopped fresh basil

1 tablespoon chopped fresh thyme

1 tablespoon chopped fresh sage

2 bay leaves

1 teaspoon salt

¼ teaspoon freshly ground pepper

Freshly grated Parmigiano-Reggiano, for garnish

1. In a large saucepan or flameproof casserole dish, heat the olive oil over medium-high heat. Add the pepper, leeks, and garlic and cook for 5 minutes, stirring frequently so garlic does not brown. Stir in the vegetable stock, tomatoes with their juice, vegetables, basil, thyme, sage, bay leaves, salt, and pepper.

2. Bring the mixture to the boil over high heat. Reduce heat to low, cover, and simmer for 30 minutes.

3. Uncover the soup and simmer for 15 to 20 minutes longer, or until the soup is of the desired consistency. To serve, remove the bay leaves and ladle the soup into bowls. Sprinkle Parmigiano-Reggiano over each serving.

SERVES 8

Marino's BLT on Rye

There are times in life when only a Marino-style sandwich will do. Marino's version, bacon and onion paired together with a perfectly ripe tomato, is accented with a quick Russian dressing concoction of mayonnaise and tomato ketchup. You be the judge. My personal recommendation is if you can find Mrs. Fanning's Bread & Butter Pickles to serve on the side, so much the better.

Kay's desire to make this healthier for Marino only results in her deciding to microwave the bacon instead of frying it. This is practically a guilt-free method for enjoying bacon without all the grease. Arrange the bacon slices on a stack of three piecesof kitchen paper on a microwaveable plate. Cover the bacon with another piece of kitchen paper. Microwave on HIGH power for 2 $\frac{1}{2}$ to 4 minutes, or until the bacon is browned and crisp.

Russian Dressing:

1 tablespoon mayonnaise or salad dressing

1 tablespoon tomato ketchup

1 teaspoon pickle relish or chopped gherkins

Sandwich:

2 large slices rye bread, toasted and kept warm

Butter, for spreading

Lettuce leaves, to serve

4 slices thick-cut bacon, cooked until crisp and well-drained

2 slices beefsteak tomato

Salt, to taste (optional)

2 slices ($1/4$ inch/6 millimetres thick) onion

1. For the Russian Dressing: in a small bowl, stir together the mayonnaise or salad dressing, tomato ketchup, and pickle relish or gherkins until blended.

2. To make the sandwich: place the toasted rye bread on a chopping board. Spread with butter, then top one of the slices with a layer of lettuce leaves. Spread half of the Russian Dressing over the lettuce. Top with the bacon and tomato slices; sprinkle the tomatoes with salt, if desired. Add the onion slices and another layer of lettuce leaves. Spread with the remaining dressing. Top with the second slice of rye bread. Cut the sandwich in half and serve.

SERVES 1

Salade de Gruyère

(Gruyère Salad)

Walking on the streets of Paris, Kay and Jay Talley, an ATF agent at Interpol, wind up at the charming Café Runtz at 16 Rue Favart (which I discovered while researching Black Notice in Paris, one of many Parisian bistros recommended by my friend Paul Elbling, the chef at La Petite France in Richmond). The bistro, which features Alsatian dishes like this Salade de Gruyère, was recently given a total makeover by star decorator Jacques Grange. Since the menu is in French, Jay, who speaks fluent French, suggests starting off with the Salade de Gruyère. The Gruyère, or Swiss cheese, on the salad looks like pasta, because it's cut into long narrow strips.

The interesting thing about this salad is that the cheese is first marinated in a white wine vinaigrette dressing, then the salad is assembled with the cheese placed on the top and the dressing spooned over. Jay chooses a Santenay red Burgundy to drink, but a Beaujolais would also be a great choice.

Dressing:

4 ounces/115 grams sliced Gruyère cheese

5 tablespoons olive oil

5 tablespoons white wine vinegar

2 tablespoons finely chopped fresh parsley

2 teaspoons Dijon mustard

½ teaspoon salt

¹/₄ teaspoon freshly ground pepper

3 ounces/85 grams finely chopped onion

Salad:

10 ounces/280 grams torn mixed salad leaves

1. For the dressing: cut the Gruyère cheese into strips that are 2 inches/5 centimetres long and ¹/₄ inch/6 millimetres wide. Arrange the cheese in a shallow bowl. In a jar with a tight-fitting lid, combine the olive oil, vinegar, parsley, mustard, salt and pepper. Shake well to combine. Add the onion to the dressing and pour over the cheese. Cover and refrigerate for at least 1 hour or up to several hours.

2. To serve the salad, arrange the salad leaves on salad plates. Using a slotted spoon, arrange the marinated cheese strips over the salads. Stir the dressing remaining from the cheese and drizzle it over each salad. Serve immediately.

SERVES 6

The Last Precinct

In the kitchen, I set the oven and cook pasta. I mix grated cheeses with ricotta and begin layering it and meat sauce between noodles in a deep dish. Anna stuffs dates with cream cheese and fills a bowl with salted nuts while Marino, Lucy and McGovern pour beer and wine or mix whatever holiday potion they want, which in Marino's case is a spicy Bloody Mary made with his moonshine.

He is in a weird mood and well on his way to getting drunk. The Tlip file is a black hole, still in the bag of presents, ironically under the Christmas tree. Marino knows what's in that file, but I don't ask him. Nobody does. Lucy begins getting out ingredients for chocolate chip cookies and two pies—one peanut butter, the other Key lime—as if we are feeding the entire city. McGovern uncorks a Chambertin Grand Cru red Burgundy while Anna sets the table, and the file pulls silently and with great force. It is as if all of us have made an unspoken agreement to at least drink a toast and get dinner going before we start talking about murder.

"Anybody else want a Bloody?" Marino talks loudly and hangs out in the kitchen doing nothing helpful. "Hey, Doc, how 'bout I mix up a pitcher?" He yanks open the refrigerator and grabs a handful of Spicy Hot V8 juices and starts popping open the small cans I wonder how much Marino had to drink before he got here and the safety comes off my anger. In the first place, I am insulted that he put the file under the tree, as if this is his idea of a tasteless, morbid joke. What is he implying? This is my Christmas present? Or is he so callous it didn't even occur to him that when he rather unceremoniously stuck the bag under the tree the file was still in it? He bumps past me and starts pressing lemon halves into the electric juicer and tosses the rinds in the sink.

"Well, I guess nobody's gonna help me so I'll just help myself," he mutters. "Hey!" he calls out as if we aren't in the same room with him. "Anybody think to buy horseradish?"

Madame Dugat's Mousse au Chocolat

(Chocolate Mousse)

Kay reminisces wistfully with her friend Anna about a trip to France that she and Benton made, remembering the wine-tasting from the casks of Dugat and Drouhin. *When I was doing research for* The Last Precinct, *I travelled extensively through the French wine country. My French publisher and I had lunch with Monsieur and Madame Dugat after touring their vineyard and wine cellar. It was an authentic French country repast, a sausage and cheese platter with, of course, different wines for sampling. For dessert, Madame Dugat presented us with her* Mousse au Chocolat, *a heavenly chocolate creation that I will never forget.*

Here is an American adaptation of that pudding, which calls for readily accessible sweet cooking chocolate. The whipping cream helps provide the proper texture for this delectable mousse. Caution: if you cannot eat foods that contain uncooked eggs, skip this pudding.

The Dugats recommend a red dessert wine, such as a Banyuls or a Maury, both made in Roussillon, France, but any light, mildly sweet red wine or red Bordeaux will do.

8 ounces/225 grams sweet cooking chocolate (not chocolate chips)

4 tablespoons water

6 very large eggs, separated

4 fluid ounces/115 millilitres whipping cream

Fresh raspberries and mint leaves, for decoration

1. Break the chocolate into small pieces and place in a heavy $1\frac{1}{2}$ pint/1-litre saucepan with the water. Melt the chocolate over low heat, stirring constantly, until it is completely melted and smooth. Remove from the heat; cool for 10 minutes.

2. In a large bowl, beat the egg yolks with an electric mixer on high speed for about 5 minutes, until thick and lemon-coloured. Beat in the chocolate mixture until blended; set aside.

3. Wash the beaters thoroughly with hot soapy water (any fat remaining on beaters will prevent the egg whites from whipping). In a large bowl, beat the egg whites on high speed until stiff peaks form. In a third bowl, beat the cream on high speed until stiff (no need to wash the beaters again).

4. With a rubber spatula, gently fold the beaten egg whites and whipped cream into the chocolate mixture with an up-and-over motion, until the mixture is thoroughly blended and no traces of white remain. Do not stir.

5. Spoon the mousse into six to eight individual dessert dishes or long-stemmed goblets, or turn the mixture into a large serving bowl. Cover and refrigerate the mousse several hours or up to overnight, until firm. To serve, decorate each serving with fresh raspberries and mint leaves.

SERVES 6 TO 8

Lucy's Favourite Chocolate Chip Surprise Cookies

n this Christmas scene from The Last Precinct, *"Lucy begins getting out ingredients for chocolate chip cookies and two pies—one peanut butter, the other Key lime—as if we are feeding the entire city."* Lucy has learned the art of intuitive cooking from her Aunt Kay, who knows that cooking at its core is an emotion. It's a way to show affection and love. And we should never get caught up in exactly how to do it, only in the fact that we should do it. (As a child growing up in Florida, I used to make cookies for all my neighbours—this recipe uses all my favourite ingredients.)

These chewy cookies are irresistible morsels for the soul. They can be made with your favourite lavish combination of chocolate and peanut butter, or white chocolate chips, or toffee bits (your choice is the surprise) and any of four kinds of nuts. Rich in oats, brown sugar, and butter, they can be made into giant-size cookies for gifts or into smaller rounds to fill up the cookie jar.

If you are tempted to double this recipe, you will get better results if you make two batches at the same time in separate bowls. Otherwise, when all the ingredients are doubled, the cookies tend to spread too much on the baking sheet.

8 ounces/225 grams butter, softened

6 ounces/170 grams soft light brown sugar

3 ounces/85 grams granulated sugar

2 very large eggs

1 tablespoon vanilla extract

12½ ounces/355 grams plain flour

6 ounces/170 grams rolled oats

1 teaspoon baking soda

½ teaspoon salt

7 ounces/200 grams semi-sweet chocolate chips

5 ounces/140 grams butterscotch, peanut butter or white chocolate
   chips, or toffee bits

5 ounces/140 grams chopped nuts, such as pecans, walnuts, peanuts or
   macadamia nuts

1. Pre-heat the oven to 375°F/190°C/gas mark 5. In a large bowl, beat to-gether the butter, light brown sugar, and granulated sugar with an electric mixer on low speed until blended. Beat in the eggs and vanilla extract until well mixed. Set aside.

2. In a medium bowl, stir together the flour, oats, baking soda, and salt. Stir the flour mixture into the butter mixture until well blended.

3. Stir in the chocolate chips, other chips of your choice, and nuts until combined. Drop the dough by rounded tablespoonfuls, 2 inches/5 centimetres apart, onto greased baking sheets.

4. Bake the cookies on the middle oven shelf for 9 to 11 minutes, or until the cookies are golden brown and set in the centre. Allow the cookies to rest on the baking sheets for 1 minute, then transfer to wire racks. When the cookies have cooled completely, store in a tightly covered container.

MAKES ABOUT 4 DOZEN COOKIES

Variation

CHOCOLATE CHIP COOKIE GIANTS: Prepare the cookie dough as directed. Drop the dough 2 ounces/55 grams at a time onto baking sheets, placing the mounds 3 inches/8 centimetres apart. Bake for 13 to 15 minutes, or until golden brown. Makes about 28 giant cookies.

Peanut Butter-Chocolate Pie

Kay cleverly puts chocolate in her peanut butter pie to avoid that pesky problem of peanut butter sticking to the roof of your mouth. She crushes chocolate wafers into the butter-crumb crust and melts some chocolate to weave into the peanut butter-honey filling. The whole creation is topped with a whipped-cream layer, sweetened with brown sugar, and dotted with chopped peanuts.

Cut the pie into small wedges to delight your dinner guests (and so they won't feel so guilty asking for seconds).

MAKE-AHEAD TIP: You can make this pie up to two days ahead, and if you have a very strong character, you may be able to forget it's in the fridge for that length of time.

SHORTCUT TIP: Purchase a 9-inch/23-centimetre pre-heated pastry case to use in place of the crust recipe. Begin making the pie at step 2.

Crust:

6 ounces/170 grams crushed chocolate wafers (about 32 biscuits)

3 ounces/85 grams butter, melted

Filling:

3 tablespoons cornflour

Pinch of salt

3 very large egg yolks

10 fluid ounces/280 millilitres milk

4 fluid ounces/115 millilitres honey

4 ounces/115 grams creamy peanut butter

2 squares (2 ounces/55 grams) unsweetened cooking chocolate,
   chopped

Topping:

8 fluid ounces/225 millilitres whipping cream

3 tablespoons soft light brown sugar

2½ ounces/70 grams chopped peanuts

1. For the crust: in a medium bowl, stir together the crumbs and melted butter until moistened. With clean hands or the back of a spoon, press the mixture onto the bottom and sides of a 9-inch/23-centimetre pie tin. Refrigerate the crust while preparing the filling.

2. For the filling: in a medium saucepan, stir together the cornflour and salt. In a small bowl, whisk together the egg yolks, milk, and honey; gradually whisk into the cornflour mixture until blended. Cook over medium heat, stirring constantly, for 3 to 5 minutes, until the mixture thickens and boils; stir constantly for 1 minute.

3. Remove the pan from the heat. Stir in the peanut butter and chocolate until the mixture is well combined and the chocolate is melted and smooth. Press a piece of greaseproof paper directly over the filling to prevent a skin from forming. Cool the mixture for 15 minutes.

4. Pour the filling into the chilled pie shell. Cover the pie with aluminium foil or cling film and refrigerate it for several hours or overnight, until firm.

5. For the topping: in a large bowl, beat the cream with an electric mixer on high speed until stiff. Sprinkle the brown sugar over the whipped cream and beat it in until blended. Spread the cream mixture over the pie. Sprinkle the peanuts over the top. Cover the pie loosely and refrigerate at least 2 hours or until ready to serve. Cut into small wedges.

MAKES ONE 9-INCH/23 CENTIMETRE PIE

Key Lime
Meringue Pie

Key lime pie is a signature dessert for many a south Florida restaurant and throughout the West Indies where Key limes, or the bottled juice, are available. Key limes are a specific hybrid of lime that's different from the common green Persian limes that are the most familiar. Small golf ball-size Key limes have yellowish green rinds and distinctively flavoured juice. (You can make this pie with fresh regular lime juice; it will simply have a different flavour.) One caveat: be sure to use regular limes for the grated zest, since the zest of Key limes can be quite bitter.

It can be difficult to find Key limes outside of Florida, but, fortunately, the juice is available bottled. One good source comes from Key West, a product called Nellie & Joe's Famous Key West Lime Juice. Go to their website at www.keylimejuice.com, or check larger supermarkets and speciality food shops in your area.

This sublime Key Lime Meringue Pie is an ethereal dessert, topped with a billowy meringue that has about as much substance as Kay's love life does most of the time. And though Kay is typically not a dessert eater, she always cleans her plate with this one. (In Miami, where I grew up, my grandmother had Key lime trees and we would squeeze the juice, freeze it, and enjoy fresh Key lime pies year-round.)

I like to serve this pie at Christmas, which gave me the idea to include it in the Christmas scene in The Last Precinct. With the pie, I always pass around Belgian chocolates. A few years ago, I had two hours off during a Belgian book tour and where did I go? I hopped in a cab to find the best

Belgian chocolates—Wittamer. Founded in 1910 by Henri Wittamer in the Grand Sablon, the fashionable quarter of art and antique shops in Brussels, Wittamer Chocolates to this day is world renowned for its stringent quality requirements and time-honoured traditional methods. (You can order Wittamer Chocolates, shipped directly from Belgium, at www.chocolatepicture.com)

Making a meringue is an easy matter of knowing how long to beat the egg whites. First, separate the whites carefully; even a trace of egg yolk in them is fat that will prevent the whites from billowing up in your mixing bowl. Use a glass or metal bowl, never plastic, and squeaky-clean beaters. If possible, allow the whites to stand at room temperature while you are making the crust and filling for the pie; that encourages better volume when you beat them. Beat the whites, adding the sugar gradually by tablespoonfuls so that it dissolves, until the whites become thick and snow white. At intervals, turn off the beaters and lift them out of the meringue—if the peaks of meringue stand up straight, the meringue is ready to use. If you see peaks, but the tips of them curl over, keep beating and testing the meringue until they stand up and salute!

Allow the pie to cool for a minimum of four hours before cutting it.

MAKE-AHEAD TIP: *Cool the pie and chill it, uncovered, until the next day.*

SHORTCUT TIP: *In place of the home-made Butter Crust, you can substitute a half package of refrigerated or frozen sweet shortcrust or dessert pastry. Follow the package directions for pre-baking a single 9-inch/23-centimetre crust. Then continue the recipe with step 4.*

Butter Crust:

8 ounces/225 grams plain flour

2 teaspoons sugar

$\frac{1}{4}$ teaspoon salt

4 ounces/115 grams cold butter, cut up

5 to 6 tablespoons iced water

Filling:

1 tin (14 fluid ounces/400 milllilitres) sweetened condensed milk

4 very large egg yolks

4 fluid ounces/115 millilitres Key lime or fresh regular lime juice

Finely grated zest of 2 limes (not Key limes)

Pinch of salt

Meringue:

4 very large egg whites

$1/4$ teaspoon cream of tartar

3 ounces/85 grams sugar

1. For the crust: in a medium bowl, stir together the flour, sugar, and salt. With a pastry blender or two knives, cut in the butter until it resembles small peas. (For helpful hints on cutting in butter, see the headnote for Mrs. McTigue's Cheddar Cheese Biscuits, page 36.) Sprinkle the water over the dough one tablespoon at a time, stirring it in until the dough comes together and leaves the side of the bowl. Turn the dough out onto a lightly floured surface or pastry board and gather it into a ball. Wrap the dough in cling film and place it in the freezer for 20 to 30 minutes, or until well chilled, but not frozen.

2. Pre-heat the oven to 400°F/200°C/gas mark 6. Knead the chilled dough about 5 times on a lightly floured surface. Flatten the dough into a disk with the palm of your hand. With a lightly floured rolling pin, roll the dough into an 11-inch/28-centimetre round. Gently fold the dough into quarters, and transfer it to a 9-inch/23-centimetre pie tin or a tart tin. Carefully unfold the

dough and ease it into the tin without stretching it. Turn the edges under and flute them, if desired or, if using a tart tin, trim the dough all around the edge of the tin.

3. To bake the crust: loosely line the pastry crust with a 12x12-inch/30x30-centimetre piece of aluminium foil; fill it with 8 ounces/225 grams of baking beans to prevent shrinkage. Bake the crust for 10 minutes. Remove the beans with the foil; bake for 6 to 8 minutes longer, or until golden brown. Transfer to a wire rack to cool.

4. For the filling: reduce the oven temperature to 325°F/170°C/gas mark 3. In a medium bowl, stir together the sweetened condensed milk, egg yolks, lime juice, lime zest, and salt until well combined. Pour the mixture into the crust. Bake for 10 minutes (the filling will be soft-set on top). Leave the oven on.

5. For the meringue: in a large bowl, beat the egg whites and cream of tartar with an electric mixer on medium speed until foamy. Beating on high speed, add the sugar, one tablespoon at a time, until the mixture forms stiff peaks.

6. With a rubber spatula, carefully spread the meringue over the hot pie, sealing it to the edges of the crust so that there are no gaps between the crust and the meringue (this prevents "weeping" and shrinkage later). Bake the meringue for 15 to 20 minutes, or until golden brown.

7. Transfer the pie to a wire rack; cool at least 4 hours before cutting and serving. If not serving it right after cooling, refrigerate the pie and serve it the next day.

MAKES ONE 9-INCH/23 CENTIMETRE PIE

Crostini di Polenta con Funghi Trifolati

(Grilled Polenta Topped with Sautéed Assorted Mushrooms)

Polenta is the Italian version of cornmeal mush, a mixture of yellow cornmeal cooked with water until it makes a thick batter. Spread in a shallow pan and then baked, fried, or grilled, the bright yellow triangles, squares, or sticks of polenta are a delightful substitute for bread or pasta in any menu.

Lumi Restaurant, an elegant, romantic regional Italian restaurant housed in a two-storey brownstone at 963 Lexington Avenue (70th Street) in New York City, is first described in a deposition scene in The Last Precinct. The former private residence is filled with comfortable tables, a fireplace, bay windows, antique mirrors, and candlelight. Chef Hido Holli likes to use fresh seasonal ingredients in his ever-changing Italian menu.

An alleged serial killer named Jean-Baptiste Chandonne is questioned about an attractive woman he met at the restaurant. In perfect Italian, he describes the polenta crostini he was enjoying, topped with assorted sautéed mushrooms and a drizzle of truffle oil. It was complemented by a 1993 Massolino Barolo, a red Italian Burgundy wine, which happens to be Kay's favourite. Any good red French Burgundy or merlot could be served with the polenta.

Chef Hido Holli and his wife, Lumi, proprietors of Lumi, were kind enough to share this recipe, along with the next two that follow. The combination of mushrooms gives the topping a mix of meaty, rich flavours. The *truffle oil, available at speciality food shops, adds a subtle, earthy flavour when drizzled over the finished dish.*

SHORTCUT TIP: Instead of making the polenta recipe as directed in step 1, purchase a box of 5-minute or quick-cook polenta. Follow the package directions for making the polenta, then continue with step 2 and the Mushroom Topping.

Polenta:

2½ pints/1.4 litres water

1 teaspoon sea salt or table salt

8 ounces/225 grams yellow cornmeal

2 tablespoons olive oil

Mushroom Topping:

3 tablespoons olive oil

12 ounces/340 grams trimmed and chopped fresh mushrooms such
    as oyster, chanterelle, portobello, or shiitake (if using portobellos
    or shiitakes, remove the stems)

2 cloves garlic, finely chopped

1 tablespoon chopped fresh rosemary, plus sprigs for garnish

1 tablespoon chopped fresh parsley

¼ teaspoon salt

Pinch of freshly ground pepper

1 tablespoon truffle oil or extra-virgin olive oil (optional)

Freshly grated Parmigiano-Reggiano, for sprinkling

1. For the polenta: in a large heavy saucepan, bring the water and salt to the boil over high heat. Gradually add the cornmeal by handfuls in a thin stream into the boiling water, stirring constantly to prevent lumps, until all

of the cornmeal has been added. Reduce the heat to low and cook the mixture, stirring constantly, for 20 to 25 minutes, until it becomes very thick and leaves the side of the pan. Remove from the heat; stir in the olive oil.

2. Line a 13x9x2-inch/33x23x5-centimetre baking tin or dish with aluminium foil; spray the foil with non-stick cooking spray or oil it lightly. Spread the cooked polenta evenly in the tin, smoothing the top with a rubber spatula. Cool for 30 minutes.

3. Twenty minutes before serving, prepare the mushroom topping: in a large frying pan, heat 2 tablespoons of the olive oil over medium-high heat. Add the mushrooms and garlic and cook, stirring frequently, for 5 minutes. Stir in the rosemary, parsley, salt, and pepper. Cook, stirring frequently, for 3 to 5 minutes longer, or until the mushrooms are deep golden brown and tender. Remove from the heat; cover and keep warm.

4. Pre-heat the barbecue to medium-hot or pre-heat the grill. Holding both ends of the foil, carefully lift the polenta from the tin onto a cutting surface. Cut the polenta into 12 to 16 triangles or rectangles (for either 6 or 8 servings); transfer the polenta to a lightly oiled grilling tray or the rack of the grill pan. Brush the polenta with the remaining 1 tablespoon of olive oil.

5. Barbecue the polenta for 8 to 10 minutes, until the slices are heated through and beginning to brown around the edges, turning once half-way through the cooking time. (Or grill the polenta 4 inches/10 centimetres from the heat source for 6 to 8 minutes, turning once.)

6. To serve, arrange 2 pieces of polenta on 6 or 8 salad or first-course plates. Spoon the warm mushroom mixture over the polenta, dividing it evenly. Drizzle the truffle oil or olive oil over each serving, if desired, and garnish with rosemary sprigs. Serve with Parmigiano-Reggiano for sprinkling on top.

SERVES 6 TO 8

Giardinietto
al Profumo di Erbe
(Grilled Garden Vegetables)

In this scene from The Last Precinct, Susan Pless orders this delicious starter/side dish while dining with Chandonne at Lumi. This dish is made from a seasonal selection of vegetables quickly grilled in a light bath of extra-virgin olive oil and fragrant fresh herbs. Choose a variety of your favourite vegetables or use whatever you have on hand. Firm vegetables, such as carrots and fennel, should be boiled or steamed first for 2 to 3 minutes to soften them a bit before finishing them off under the grill.

It's amazing how grilling brings out the sweet, subtle flavours of different vegetables. This simple dish is the perfect accompaniment to grilled or roasted meats, salmon, or chicken. If you don't have a large grill, grill the vegetables in batches, then grill your entrée. It's fine if the vegetables are served just warm or at room temperature. Any cold leftovers, if you are lucky enough to have them, are excellent the next day, tossed into a salad.

2 pounds/900 grams assorted vegetables, cut into $\frac{1}{4}$-inch/6-millimetre-
thick slices or sticks (peeled aubergine; blanched, trimmed fennel;
blanched, peeled carrot, courgette, or summer squash; shiitake
mushroom caps; portobello mushroom caps; chicory; yellow, red,
or green pepper; or trimmed asparagus spears)

2 plum tomatoes, quartered lengthwise

4 spring onions, trimmed

4 tablespoons olive oil

1 tablespoon chopped fresh thyme

1 teaspoon chopped fresh rosemary

1 teaspoon chopped fresh sage

1 teaspoon chopped fresh oregano

1 teaspoon salt

1 1/2 teaspoons freshly ground pepper

Freshly grated Parmigiano-Reggiano, for sprinkling

1. Pre-heat the barbecue to medium-hot or pre-heat the grill. On a lightly oiled grilling tray or on the rack of a grill pan arrange the vegetables in a single layer. Whisk together olive oil, herbs, salt, and pepper. Drizzle mixture over the vegetables. (Or toss the vegetables with the oil mixture and grill them in batches, if necessary.)

2. Barbecue for 5 to 8 minutes, or until the vegetables are nearly tender. (Or grill 4 inches/10 centimetres from the heat source for 5 to 7 minutes.) Serve hot or at room temperature, sprinkled with Parmigiano-Reggiano.

SERVES 4

Costolette di Agnello alle Sette Erbe

(Lamb Chops Seasoned with Seven Herbs)

This roasted rack of lamb from Lumi is one of the easiest, most elegant dishes you can make in just about an hour from start to finish. To make this dish successfully, it's wisest to order two racks of baby lamb that have been trimmed and "Frenched", with the backbone of the rack removed, to make carving them easy.

"Frenching" a rack of lamb means trimming the meat and fat from the rib bones so that they are exposed. Each rack will contain seven to eight ribs. Each lamb chop has only a small nugget of succulent meat on it, allowing for just 2 to 2½ servings per rack. Larger racks weighing up to 2 pounds/900 grams will provide 3 servings per rack. (Increase the roasting time, using 30 minutes per 1 pound/450 grams as a guide for medium-rare.)

Before roasting, if necessary, trim away everything but a thin layer of the fat that's covering the meaty end of the rack. The seasoning is a simple herb rub composed of seven fresh herbs. If only three or four of the fresh herbs are available, simply double the amount of each herb, and rub the mixture generously over the fat side of the racks.

Chef Hido Holli serves the lamb with three side dishes: aubergine, artichoke, and asparagus. Included here is a simple treatment for a grilled asparagus accompaniment. You can also serve this entrée with Hido's polenta (page 212) or add some boiled new potatoes, tossed with melted butter and herbs. Pour a good red Bordeaux or pinot noir wine to drink.

Lamb:

1 teaspoon chopped fresh flat-leaf parsley

½ teaspoon chopped fresh rosemary, plus leaves for garnish

½ teaspoon chopped fresh thyme

½ teaspoon chopped fresh oregano, plus leaves for garnish

½ teaspoon chopped fresh tarragon

½ teaspoon chopped fresh basil

½ teaspoon chopped fresh sage

2 racks (7 to 8 ribs each, about 1¼ to 1½ pounds/565 to 675 grams each) lamb, trimmed of fat and "Frenched"

Salt and freshly ground pepper

Grilled Asparagus:

1 pound/450 grams fresh asparagus, trimmed

1 to 2 tablespoons olive oil

Salt and freshly ground pepper

2 tablespoons balsamic vinegar

Freshly grated Parmigiano-Reggiano, for sprinkling

1. For the lamb: pre-heat the oven to 375°F/190°C/gas mark 5. In a small bowl, mix together all the herbs. Rub the herb mixture over the meaty side of the lamb; season with salt and pepper. Place the lamb racks, meaty side up, on a rack in a shallow roasting tin. Insert a meat thermometer into the meatiest part of the roast, not touching the bone.

2. Roast for 30 to 40 minutes, or until thermometer registers about 130°F/54°C for medium-rare (temperature will rise about 5°F/1 to 2°C after roast is removed from the oven). Cover the roast and let stand for 5 minutes before carving.

3. For the asparagus: while the meat is roasting, pre-heat the barbecue to medium-hot or pre-heat the grill. Arrange the asparagus on a grilling tray or

on a rack in the grill pan. Brush with the olive oil and sprinkle with salt and pepper. Grill for about 5 minutes, until asparagus is nearly tender, turning the spears once after 2 minutes. (Or grill 4 inches/10 centimetres from the heat source for about 5 minutes.) Transfer the asparagus to a platter and drizzle the vinegar over it. Sprinkle with Parmigiano-Reggiano.

4. Carve the lamb rack by cutting between the ribs into individual chops. Arrange the chops on each dinner plate and garnish with fresh herb sprigs. Serve immediately with the asparagus.

| SERVES 4 TO 5 |

Index

Note

Both metric and imperial measurements are given for the recipes. Follow either set of measures, not a mixture of both, as they are not interchangeable.

All spoon measurements are level unless otherwise stated. Sets of measuring spoons are available in metric and imperial for accurate measurement of small quantities.

Resources

Items in the photographs not credited are privately owned.

Page 17, Kay's Stew with Red Wine and Garlic: Vietri Cucina Fresca square casserole and wire basket from Sur La Table. Le Jacquard Francais "Abecedaire" teatowel from Malibu Colony Company. Wine from Wally's Wine & Spirits.

Page 18, *Zuppa di Aglio Fresco*: Cottura "Pompeii" bowl and plate from BoDanica.

Page 19, *Tortellini Verdi*: "Beyrle" plate by Sud & Company from Salutations Home. Sabre flatware from Maison Sud.

Page 20, *Salade de Gruyère*: "Noisette" pewter flatware, salt and pepper shakers, and French tumbler from Maison Sud. Reidel stemware from Wally's Wine & Spirits.

Page 21, Madame Dugat's *Mousse au Chocolat*: Antique silver tray courtesy of The Bissell House Bed & Breakfast. Silver filigree Italian compotes from Maison Sud. White hem-stitched cocktail napkins from Salutations Home. Dessert wine from Larchmont Wine & Spirits.

Page 22, Italian Sausage Pizza with Peppers, Mushrooms and Onions: Cottura "Animali Birds" dinner plate.

Page 23, Mrs. McTigue's Cheddar Cheese Biscuits: Spode "Stafford Flowers" porcelain compote, Nay et Al napkin, Waterford "Lismore" decanter and port wine glasses all from Geary's. Warwick oval tray from Room with a View.

Page 24, Fresh Fruit Salad with Blood Orange Dressing: Mottahedeh "Merian" dinner plate and cup and saucer from Jimmy K's. Kirk & Matz silver tea strainer from Jensen-Young. Sferra Bros. "Madeira" hand-embroidered placemat and napkin from Shaxted. Sferra Bros. "Venice Lace" boudoir pillow from Room with a View. Ives Delorme "Triomphe" quilted sham and blanket cover from Malibu Colony Company. Labrazel antique gold "Classico" bed tray from Linens et Al or www.Labrazel.com. Italian filigree champagne flute and "Noisette" pewter flatware from Maison Sud.

Page 97, Grilled Grouper with Butter and Key Lime Juice: "Torsade Ivory" flatware by Zrike.

Page 99, *Pollo al Limone*: Plate and glass from Sur La Table. Vertu "Rooster" tile coasters from Maison Sud. Wine from Wally's Wine & Spirits.

Page 100, Pork Loin with Fig and Prosciutto Stuffing: Hand-painted Italian platter and pewter carving set from Maison Sud. Illume candles from Illume.

Page 101, *Crostini di Polenta con Funghi Trifolati*: Mottahedeh Italian majolica square tray from The Blue House.

Page 102, Jack Daniel's Chocolate-Pecan Pie: Emile Henry pie plate from Sur La Table.

Page 103, Veal Breast Stuffed with Spinach Pistou: Mottahedeh "Festival Red" charger from Room with a View. Le Jacquard Francais "Palazzo" tablecloth from Malibu Colony Company. Cottura antique reproduction vase.

Page 104, Lasagne with Marinara Sauce and Porcini Mushrooms: Wines from Wally's Wine & Spirits.

Page 105, Greek Salad with Red Wine Vinaigrette: Annieglass "Rock" salad bowl from LG Gallery. Nutmeg pewter salad servers by Sally Richards.

Page 106, Rose's Vegetable Soup with Italian Herbs: Cottura "Garofano" soup tureen. Lace tablecloth courtesy of The Bissell House Bed & Breakfast.

Page 108, *Le Pappardelle del Cantunzein*: Cottura "Geometrico" platter.

Page 109, Barbecued Baby Back Ribs: Beer mug and denim napkin from Sur La Table.

Page 110, Wild Rice Salad with Cashews: Provence wine glass from Maison Sud. Sferra Bros. Hem-stitched linen napkin from Shaxted.

Page 111, Fruit-Marinated Lamb Kebabs: Pewter charger and napkin ring from Salutations Home. Rattan vase and wine coaster from Upstairs at Diamond. Sabre flatware from Maison Sud. Pewter salt and pepper shakers from Sur La Table. "Aspen" leaf skewers by Janet Torelli from Tesoro. Reidel stemware and wine from Wally's Wine & Spirits.

Page 112, *Lasagne coi Carciofi*: Royal Worcester "Contrast" dinner plate from David Orgel. Mottahedeh charcoal "Festival" charger from Panache of La Jolla. "Acropole" flatware by Zrike.

Page 114, Braided Country Bread: Kitchen towel, Terramoto mixing bowls, and decorative bottles from Sur La Table.

Page 115, Jumbo Shrimps with Bev's Kicked by a Horse Cocktail Sauce: Sea motif cocktail picks from Sur La Table.

Page 116, New York Steaks with Red Wine Marinade: Cottura "Quartieri" dinner plate from BoDanica. "Antique Rope" flatware from Pottery Barn.

Page 117, Classic English Breakfast: Rustic French buffet plate and cup and saucer from Salutations Home. Toast rack from Sur La Table. Antique salt and pepper set and flatware courtesy of The Bissell House Bed & Breakfast.

Page 118, Omelette with Sweet Peppers and Onions: BIA "Sienna" dinner plate. Le Jacquard Francais "Ispahan" tablecloth from Malibu Colony Company. Etched grape pattern wine glass from Maison Sud. Wine from Wally's Wine & Spirits.

Page 119, Marino's Breakfast Bagel Sandwich: Spode "Mansard" plate from Janus. Antiques courtesy of The Bissell House Bed & Breakfast.

Page 120, *Rigatoni con Broccolo*: Annieglass "Tuscan Braid" salad bowl from Geary's.

Page 121, Shrimp Sauté with Garlic and Lemon: Silver charger and martini glasses from Sur La Table. Janet Torelli "Aspen" leaf martini pick, "Gingko Leaf" sterling tongs and "Objects Pointus" flatware by Sasaki from Tesoro.

Page 122, *Costolette di Agnello alle Sette Erbe*: Plate from Sur La Table. Zrike "Rococo" wood-handled flatware. Reidel stemware from Wally's Wine & Spirits. Chair courtesy of The Bissell House Bed & Breakfast.

Page 123, *Giardinietto al Profumo di Erbe*: Janet Torelli "Gingko Leaf" sterling silver tongs from Tesoro.

Page 124, Grilled Chicken Caesar Salad: Nancy Calhoun "Delmar Sand" plate from Pottery Shack. Dransfield & Ross napkin from Statements. Les Etains pewter fork from Maison Sud. Wine glass and pewter salt and pepper shakers from Sur La Table. Table courtesy of The Bissell House Bed & Breakfast.

Page 125, Key Lime Meringue Pie: Antique silver tea service, tiered server, and green glass plates courtesy of The Bissell House Bed & Breakfast. Hobnail cakestand by L.E. Smith.

Page 126, Ravioli with Squash and Chestnut Filling: Cottura "Geometrico" pasta bowl.

Page 127, Fig, Melon and Prosciutto Salad: Le Jacquard Francais "Andalousie" napkin from Malibu Colony Company.

Page 128, Linguine with Olive Oil, Parmesan and Onion: Riverside glass plate from Soho.